RAISING THE ECHOES

by
D.J. Fleming

Line
One
publishing ltd

ISBN 0 907036 19 8

Published by
Line One Publishing Limited
Bayshill House
Bayshill Road
Cheltenham
Glos.
GL50 3AA

CONTENTS

INTRODUCTION

The men and locomotives of Bristol, Bath Road were responsible for the many passenger duties which once existed during the steam era, and this book covers that era; 'Castles', 'Kings', 'Halls' and 'Counties' being an everyday sight. The depot's duties varied from mileage work to the once numerous local passenger and pilot duties, a wide variety of work with a wide variety of locomotives being used. This volume deals with the 1934 shed, although mention is made of the former Bristol and Exeter shed which once occupied the site.

I was much assisted with this collection of memories, with my plea for help being answered by both retired and active railwaymen, some of which are employed at the present Bath Road Diesel Depot. They were only too pleased to give me their time and tell me their stories. I would like to thank the following for their kindness, their help making this book possible. Enginemen R.A. Hacker, D. Gardner and C. Brown (Weymouth). Retired railwaymen J. Gullis, M. Channings, N. Anderson, W.E. Brean, I. Phillips, F. Hodgson, A. Barnes, and F. Thatcher. The late C.C.W. Iles and F. May. Present Gloucester diesel depot foreman D. Jones and ex Wells locoman Whittaker. I would also like to thank Rod Shippobotham for searching through old magazines for information and all photographers whose prints are used herein.

I would also like to express my gratitude to fellow author L.C. Jacks for his encouragement and his wife Mary for all the hard work and many hours spent at the typewriter preparing my manuscript. Last but not least I must thank my long suffering mother who after hearing nothing but railway talk for years must be as capable of packing the glands on a pannier tank as she is of cooking the Sunday lunch. I would like to dedicate this book to the countless Bath Road railway men past, present and future.

Chapter 1

EARLY IMPRESSIONS

My earliest memory of Bristol Bath Road shed was from the top deck of a Bristol bus. My parents and I were off on a shopping spree. As we passed over the railway bridge I noticed the line of engines waiting patiently on the coal road. My young eyes peered eagerly through the bus window, then the whole scene was blotted out by a cloud of steam that billowed from the under side of the bridge. Looking back I was, perhaps too young to appreciate my first meeting with the depot. But I recall a feeling of excitement which ran through me. It was as if an invisible finger was beckoning me to take a closer look, the year was 1947 and the four railway companies were still operating as private enterprises. The following year they would become one united body, British Railways, and I would become a train spotter.

Victoria Park became my favourite haunt, it was summertime, butterflies displayed their bright colours amongst the flower beds, legions of daddy long legs roamed the grass, the sun shone down and the atmosphere was alive with the sound and smell of steam.

In those early days of nationalisation the GWR was little altered. The locomotives were still in their green livery, they still carried stenciled shed codes on their frames and their tanks and tender sides were still lettered G.W.R. or even Great Western.

Those early memories are still quite fresh in my mind *Knight of the Thistle* taking the avoiding line with an excursion, a vision of polished paint and dazzling brass work; *Prince Henry* running tender first to Malago Sidings - I remember writing the name *Knight of the Grand Cross* carefully into my note book, all twenty one letters of it. Her huge nameplate almost extending from one side of the running plate to the other. *The Somerset Light Infantry* on the west bound express, 2846 rattling along with 60 wagons of coal behind her tender, or one of the old double bar panniers heading for Cannons Marsh Yard in the mid evening, will long be treasured memories of yester-year.

The old Standard Goods class were regulars on the scene, although mainly employed on goods duties in the St. Philips Marsh transfer link they were still very active. During both world wars they had seen a great deal of work on foreign soil. Many had remained abroad after the last war. The shrill cries of their whistles had been heard in such unlikely places as China, and even behind the Iron Curtain. One sunny afternoon I watched with great interest as a locomotive came around the bend from the St. Philips Marsh area. She puffed her way sedately towards me. I had never seen a locomotive type like

Grange class 4-6-0, 6835 Eastham Grange at Bristol Temple Meads station, in ex works condition, 4th May 1961. (D.K. Jones)

this before, her deep frames almost covered her wheels, she had an elegant look about her. As she came closer I could read the number on her front buffer-beam, the faded gold numbers read 3400. As she passed by, my eyes were open wide with wonder, her crescent shaped nameplate proudly read *Winnipeg*. Her coupling rods glinted in the sunlight and she was gone to an unknown destination. For me it was a momentous occasion, I had spotted my first 'Bulldog' class. That grand old lady had been built by Swindon craftsmen in 1904, and now she was living out her last days. The 'Bulldogs' were now a rarity in the Bristol region, they were a dying breed.

General view of Swindon Works, as seen from the water tower on 14th April 1949.

(Seaton Phillips)

A class of old timers which escaped my eyes in the local area was the 'Duke' class, but during a visit to Swindon Works I was able to see the last of the line. Standing in the yard that day in a rather forlorn condition was No. 9089. I climbed on to her footplate, her regulator and reverser handles were covered with a thin film of rust, her firebox was cold and empty, never again would she raise steam for she had come to keep a date with the cutters torch. She had given the GWR fifty four years of service, soon she would be just another memory.

The Swindon Works open days always proved to be a great success. The line of enthusiasts waiting for admission would stretch from the works entrance almost back to the railway station. As we awaited for the appointed time to arrive, so the excitement grew. Recent withdrawals and new engine

Another view, dated January 1952, showing Swindon Works yard with 5073 Blenheim, Castle class 4-6-0 and BR Standard 4-6-0 75017 by the turntable. Far right a ROD and a 28xx 2-8-0 undergo steam tests. *(Seaton Phillips)*

construction would be discussed. Then at last we would walk along the tunnel to that hallowed spot of Swindon 'A' shop. Such visits always held me spell bound. The hum of the lathes, the shower from the glowing rivets, the atmosphere of activity that filled the air. Brand new 'Halls' and 'Manors' awaiting their first tests, could all be examined from close quarters.

Engines from the Taff Vale, the Rhymney and the Brecon and Merthyr Railways could all be seen in the works yard. These and other railways had helped to make the Great Western even greater when they were absorbed into the GWR network in 1922. The amalgamation period at Swindon must have been a fantastic time, types never seen before arrived at the works from many parts. They were "Swindonised" and returned home in their new guises. Some were beyond repair and were condemned, these ended their days at the Rodburn end of the works in the scrap yard, a long way from their native Welsh Valleys.

Swindon Junction Station also had its own delights, one of my favourite pastimes was to watch the through express trains pass through the station. As far as the eye could see all the appropriate signals would be pulled off to clear, then from the works end the shrill call of the 'GWR' whistle telling all and sundry to stand back would turn our heads. The 'Castle' class at the head of the train would come into view, swaying from side to side and travelling at great speed. She would come through the station with a mighty roar, her coupling rods flashing, the exhaust blasting from her chimney. There would be a mirror like glare of polished copper and brass, the swirling dust and pieces of

8

wastepaper would flee from her path, the familiar rhythm of the carriage wheels would sing out her departure. Such were the pleasures of the visits to Swindon, the railway town.

My first visit to Bristol Temple Meads Station was in the early fifties. This also gave me my first close up view of Bath Road Shed. The downside platforms, numbers four and five gave one an excellent view of the depot. An assortment of engines were assembled in the yard. 'Stars' and 'Saints' mingled with 'Kings', 'Castles' and 'Halls', 41xx, and 55xx and panniers being prepared for their next duties rubbed shoulders with 'Granges' and Moguls in this smokey atmosphere. I would have been quite content to stand there all day, but the busy station had other attractions to offer.

General view of Bristol Bath Road depot from Temple Meads station, 9th July 1960.

(D.H. Ballantyne)

As far as railways were concerned Bristol was certainly the gateway to the West, playing host to engines from Laira, Exeter, Newton Abbot, Taunton and Penzance, Salop, Stafford Road, Old Oak Common, Ebbw Junction, Canton and many others. One Salop duty which comes to mind was train number 208. This was the 9.10am Liverpool to Plymouth which arrived at Bristol in the early afternoon and the locomotive at the train's head was a picture to behold. The motive power generally consisted of a 'County' or a 'Castle'.

Regulars on this duty during this period being, 5004 *Llanstephan Castle*, 5050 *Earl of St. Germans*, 1016 *County of Hants*, 1017 *County of Hereford* and rather appropriately 1026 *County of Salop*. These locomotives were turned out in immaculate condition, a real credit to the staff at Coleham Shed.

County class 4-6-0, 1011 County of Chester, resplendant in BR lined green livery at Swindon shed, 21st April 1957. She was to become the last survivor of her class, but falling to the cutter's torch in March 1965

(N.E. Preedy)

My first visit to Bath Road Shed was in the summer of 1950. A friend who lived close to my home had a relation who worked at the depot as a fitter and he kindly offered to give us a conducted tour on his next rest day. I was very excited at our prospects to say the least. On the appointed day we set off armed with note books etc., and the eagerness in our steps soon took us to our destination. It gave me a great thrill to walk through the shed gate without being questioned and to descend the steps into the yard below. A 'Hall' was being prepared on number 1 road, her driver who was busily engaged with his oiling duties paid us no heed as we headed for the shed.

The interior of an engine shed has its own special atmosphere. Shafts of sunlight penetrate the shadows, the locomotives take on a grey hue in the dim light. Particles of dust can be seen in the beams of sunlight, the cause of this disturbance coming from the shed sweeper who is busy at work with his brush and his number seven shovel keeping the pits and walk ways clear of ashes, soot and clinker. At the far end of the shed we had our first treat in store. Tucked away in the corner of number 1 road 2931 *Arlington Court* was receiving some attention from the fitting staff.

I had seen many of the 'Saint' class from the platform level but never before had I seen one from the ground. Her 6ft 8½in driving wheels towered above me, her oil encrusted coupling rods seemed to be of huge proportions to my young and eager eyes. This elderly lady was nearing her retirement. She had been built at Swindon in 1911, had seen service on main line express work, and survived two world wars. Once her copper and brass work had gleamed, and she had been the 'pride of the line'. Now her days were numbered, she

Saint class 4-6-0, 2945 Hillingdon Court in the yard at Bath Road, 19th August 1951.
(D.H. Ballantyne)

11

was covered in grime, her brass work was black. I picked up a piece of oily waste from the floor and gave her frame a loving rub over. Through the dirt the letters B.R.D. appeared.

How I wish that I could have spent the day just grooming her, polishing her until she shone, helping to restore her to her former glory, to the proud old lady she really was. But what would British Railways have thought of a ten year old boy climbing over one of their locomotives, I shuddered to think. I asked our guide if I could climb onto her footplate, when he said "yes", I could not climb those steps to that hallowed ground fast enough. Whilst he conversed with his mates on such mundane matters as to what Bristol City would be doing on Saturday or what won the 2.30 at Ascot, I was in seventh heaven. I studied her controls and leaned over the cab side just like the real enginemen did. Our guide told me it was time to move on. His words shattered my world of dreams for 2931 and I were hammering down to Plymouth with twelve coaches behind the tender.

The following February *Arlington Court* was sent home to Swindon for scrapping. Until then she remained at Bath Road carrying on with her duties. The other members of the 'Saint' class allocated to Bath Road during 1950 were, 2939 *Croome Court*, 2948 *Stackpole Court* and 2950 *Taplow Court*. They were withdrawn on the following dates; 2939 December 1950; 2948 November 1951 and 2950 September 1952. Most of the other 29xxs in existence at this time visited Bristol. We saw them on running-in duties from Swindon and very smart they looked in their British Railways lined black livery. One regular visitor to St. Philips Marsh Shed was old 2981 *Ivanhoe* which was frequently used on the Banbury goods duty.

The final survivor, 2920 *Saint David* went to the wall in January 1954. Many regretted the passing of these gallant engines and it is a great pity that not one was preserved. Our next treat was a conducted tour of a 45xx class engine. These delightful little tankies were employed with their 55xx sisters on local traffic around Bristol. There were twenty seven examples of the 45xx/55xx allocated to Bath Road at this period.

Out in the yard a 'County' and a 'Castle' were standing side by side, the black, mixed traffic livery of the former contrasting with the green livery of the 'Castle'. Our guide then lead us towards the disposal road and we made our way past heaps of ashes and piles of clinker, some of the larger pieces were still glowing. The smell of sulphur was caught and carried on the breeze. The first engine on the line was 4034 *Queen Adelaide*, her blower was hard on, the fire dropper was hard at work on her, and as we walked past her the last of the glowing ashes were being shovelled from her firebox. The blower was eased, the fire dropper took a roll-up from his tobacco tin and took a well deserved break.

Behind the 'Queen' was another member of the "Royal Family" his Majesty himself, No. 6000 *King George V.* The sun glinted on the bell. a momento of the successful trip to the U.S.A. The 'King' was in spotless condition, patiently waiting to be serviced and quietly gurgling to himself. Only hours earlier he had come racing down from London, his crew had booked off duty and gone home, and soon the 'King' was to enter the shed and rest himself.

We made our way to the loco factory, and as we entered the coalfield I became aware of the sound of a locomotive hard at work. As one man, we turned and watched 4535 storming the coal stage incline with six wagons of coal behind her bunker. She came to rest at the top of the grade just beneath the cast iron sign that read "Engines must not pass the arch". The brakes on the wagons were pinned down, and the loco uncoupled. She cautiously descended the bank and waited for a clear exit.

The workshop held two locomotives. 4143 and a St. Philips Marsh 77xx both of which were receiving attention from the fitters. All too soon our visit was over, our guide telling us it was time to head for home. Reluctantly we followed him across the yard. *Queen Adelaide* had moved under the coal stage, the tip clattered into life, the coal rumbled into her tender and a small cloud of black dust rose into the air. We climbed the steps and the 'County' went off shed as I closed the gate behind me. The notebook in my pocket had recorded all that we saw on that eventful day.

Unless one held a permit for visiting an engine shed, Bath Road could prove to be practically impregnable. All three "Entrances" held problems for the enthusiast who had visions of "bumping around" the depot. It was completely out of the question to just walk off one of the platform ends at Temple Meads. The shed gate situated in Bath Road also had its problems, there was generally a gateman on duty. There was one way of gaining entry, but this was not for the faint hearted, at the rear of the shed is May Walk. This was the well trodden path used by hundreds of railway men and enthusiasts alike and was the favourite route to St. Philips Marsh shed.

At the bottom of this walk just beneath the high wall of the railway institute is a set of railings. The usual Great Western cast iron sign which warns that trespassers will be prosecuted is bolted to this obstacle. After scaling these railings (not the fastest of tasks) one had to clamber down the river bank and pass beneath the railway bridge (a lot safer than crossing the lines). It was not uncommon to come face to face with a sizeable water rat or to disturb the pigeons that resided there, after dodging their missiles and clearing the assault course it was then just a matter of creeping into the rear of the shed. I was evicted from the premises on more than one occasion — it was a lot safer to purchase a one penny platform ticket and enjoy the sights from the station platform even if not quite so rewarding.

During the summer season numerous excursions passed through Bristol heading for the sun and the beaches of the West Country. A great deal of this traffic was diverted at North Somerset Junction and travelled along the Bristol avoiding lines. The school summer holidays attracted literally hundreds of train spotters to Temple Meads Station and this, plus the increase in traffic must have given the authorities quite a headache. Naturally these followers of steam took advantage of the downside platform, which in common with the others had a water column situated there.

Most of the spotters kept at a safe distance when an engine stopped for water, but of course there is always that one stubborn fellow who is the exception to the rule. For such immovable obstacles there was a simple yet most effective cure. After the engine had replenished her tank the column would be swung clear with the water just turned on. It would swing through the air sending water in all directions and 'drowning' anyone in the vicinity. The chain would hit the post with a resounding smack sending our now wet friend scuttling away in fright. Such unmovers never came back for a second helping.

Train spotters fell into several categories. First, there was the beginner who had nothing more than a sixpenny notebook and a stump of a pencil and could afford little else. At the opposite end of the scale was the fellow who had all the Ian Allan reference books (ABC's), a camera, binoculars, an impressive array of badges pinned to his lapels and was a fully paid up member of the well known and much respected Ian Allan Locospotters Club. Many of them were well travelled and tales could be heard of their many visits to depots throughout the country.

Being a relative newcomer to the scene I would sit with them on a station trolley and listen to the stories they told. These stories conjured up for me the fascinations of the different sheds on the GWR network. Tales could be heard of Old Oak Common crammed with 'Castles' and 'Kings' or of the activities of Newton Abbot on a summer Saturday. Others preferred to reminisce with stories of the Severn Tunnel Junction packed with grime encrusted 28xxs, RODs and 3150 class Prairie Tanks.

I would become enthralled with the description of the Cardiff Valley sheds many of these stories related to the Sabbath when practically everything was on shed. Lines of the Taff Vale 'A' and '04' engines and gleaming 56xxs could all be seen in my minds eye. The peace and tranquility of Abercynon and Ferndale with just the far off sound of Welsh voices united in song in the nearby chapel was not hard to imagine. The delights of the Swansea Dock Sheds were very topical with the story tellers. This was the home of the saddle tanks of Swansea Harbour Trust and Powlesland and Mason origin. All the members of the 1101 class were allocated to Danygraig. This was also the home shed of that lovely little engine built by Pecketts here in Bristol, No. 1 *Hercules*.

Trips to Fishguard, Oswestry and Croes Newydd were all vividly described.

14

No.1016 County of Hants with the 9.10am Liverpool - Plymouth at Temple Meads, with typical youthful enthusiasts of the period. *(Author)*

To me it was a case of far away places with strange sounding names. I would have to wait until I was older before I could visit such places and enjoy the fascinations myself. I remember one spotter telling me of one such trip to Gresty Lane. This was the GWR shed at Crewe. He had travelled there to spot one certain engine, only to find upon his arrival that she had been despatched to Swindon Works for repair. Such were the joys of train spotting.

Some preferred the Midland Region, but most were worshippers of the Western. Whatever their beliefs were, they all had one common interest - the steam locomotive. The majority were well behaved, damage to railway property being a rarity. As the summer season closed I would take great interest in watching the trains go home. There was a hint of sadness in the air, we would not see some of the engines again until next summer, some of the older types would be withdrawn, but we would have our memories of them. For the passengers in those trains it was also a sad event. It was the end of their holidays. They would return to their places of work, the holiday snapshots would be shown to their friends and relatives. Their sun tan would slowly disappear as they carried on with their labours in the offices, the shops and the factories. Many of them would return next year. They would work hard and save for another fortnight of bliss on the sunny beaches of the west.

The name 'excursion' was certainly a magic word at most depots. The engines employed on these duties were turned out in spotless condition. The Oxley and Pontypool Road 'Granges' and the Tyseley based 'Halls' all glinted in the sun. The various accents of the engine crews and the travellers alike all helped to add a touch of colour to the scene. During such busy periods anything on wheels was pressed into service. I distinctly remember Mogul 6361 at the head of a thirteen coach return excursion to Hirwaun. The efforts of this twenty seven year old lady up Stapleton Road Bank must have been valiant to say the least.

The fifties period saw the arrival of several new designs of locomotives to the scene. Two such arrivals come instantly to mind. The first of these occurrences was on a summer's day in 1950. A strange whistling sound filled the air, a large black slab sided locomotive vibrated to a halt on the Temple Meads downside platform. The first of the gas turbines had arrived. The year of 1951 saw the introduction of the British Railways Standard Class locomotives. The 'Britannias' made an impressive sight to us when they graced our city with their first visits. The first of these to catch my eye was 70018 *Flying Dutchman*. The first thing I noticed was her close resemblance to a London Midland engine. She was very lengthy, she had a high running plate, smoke deflectors and her driving position was on the left hand side. Her safety valves burst into life like a 'Jubilee' or a class Five. The oval plate bolted to her front end gave the game away, it read "Built Crewe".

She and her sisters had been designed at Derby Works by R.A. Riddles who was the man responsible for the Austerity class locomotives, those clanging ungraceful old ladies that had given service in many parts during those grim wartime days. 70018 looked every inch a thing of power. Although she had a strong Midland flavour about her the name she carried was of Great Western origin. *Flying Dutchman* was carried by one of the graceful 3001 class back in 1892 and had been the name of the London—Bristol Express introduced in 1862. This was the 11.45 am which eventually travelled through to Exeter. When this train was first introduced it travelled at the highest speed then known for any type of transport. It was later accelerated to arrive at Plymouth via Bristol 6¼ hours after leaving Paddington.

I thought it was a nice touch of tradition seeing such an old name on a brand new locomotive. In turn we saw all the 'Brits' allocated to the Western Region (Nos. 70015-29). The traditional names continued, *Ariel, Vulcan, Royal Star* etc., Some of these names going right back to the grass roots of the GWR. Temple Meads looked on with her stoney face and remained unmoved for she had witnessed generations of new engines during her lifetime.

Evening time at Temple Meads would find me on number nine platform. This would be my grandstand for watching the departure of the various goods trains from the low level yard. Some of the principal trains were the 7.35 Chester, the 8.45 Acton, the 9.15 Oxley and the 12.35 Carmarthen. A variety of locomotive stock could be seen on these duties, 'Halls', 'Granges', 28xxs, 47xxs, 63xxs and even the occasional 'Castle'. Regarding the departure of passenger trains the two Regions which used the station had their own

16

special style. The weather could also change the scene quite dramatically.

It is a wintery Sunday evening, the icey wind blows down the platform. The waiting passengers stamp their feet in an effort to keep warm. The less hardy variety huddle round the warmth of an inviting waiting-room fire. Through the gloom I see a red tail-light creeping towards me. The rumble of the coaches become louder, causing passengers to look up. The train has backed down from the Midland Region carriage sidings at Barrow Road, cautiously it enters the station and shudders to a halt. People appear from the shadows, forget the misery of the cold and board the train.

The motive power can vary at it's head. Tonight it is a grimey 'Black 5' from Holbeck shed. Steam escapes from numerous leaky joints obscuring her cab side number. There is a glare as her firebox doors are opened. I cannot see the fireman because the Midland engines had doors between their cabs and tenders. The shovel digs in the coal, clangs on the shoe, and thuds into the firebox. This action will be carried out again and again before the train leaves. This is known as a 'Derby charge'.

The black smoke rises from her chimney, it is caught by the wind and blows across the goods yard. Her safety valves burst into life catching some unwary passengers off guard, a shaft of steam shoots up into the beams of the station roof. Her injector gurgles, she is ready. A green light appears ahead, from the end of the platform a whistle is blown. The driver gives a blast on the whistle, the regulator is opened and with her unmistakeable bark the Class Five bursts into life. She gets to grips with her train and gets her head down for the climb up Fishponds Bank. The sound of her exhaust becomes fainter as the now brisk running train disappears into the night leaving the station as cold and bleak as it was before.

On other occasions a gleaming 'Jubilee' class could be seen standing in the old part of the station. The smell of cleaning oil burning on her smokebox, *Leander, Galatea, Kempenfelt* or *Shovel* all once the pride of Barrow Road Shed. Sometimes a visitor from Carlisle Kingmoor or Canklow could be seen working their way home. The delights of an ageing Compound or a lovely class 2MT will be treasured memories for many years to come.

A change of season and a different Region takes us to platform nine, the coaches await the arrival of the locomotive. The distorted voice of the station announcer gives the necessary information. Shafts of sunlight penetrate the shady interior. Trolleys rumble along the platform, a porter whistles a popular song as he goes about his duties. There is a scream of flanges from the platform end, a 'Castle' class is backing on to her train. The band of trainspotters watch every move as she glides by. The fireman leaves the footplate and drops down behind the engine to couple up. There is the familiar cry of "Ease up", the coupling clangs on the hook, the vacuum pipes are connected. The fireman walks to the front of his steed, drops the lamp on the bracket, and rejoins his mate on the footplate.

The final minutes tick away on the station clock, the driver opens the ejector sending a hollow sound up the 'Castle's' chimney. She is gleaming, a picture of burnished copper and brass. The smell of steam and warm oil is pleasing to the nostrils. The highly polished crescent shaped nameplate proudly shows everyone she was Christened *Dorchester Castle,* her safety valve simmers, gradually increasing in sound until an eruption of white steam rises towards the heavens. A whistle blows, the right away is passed from man to man down the curving platform. The familiar blast of a Western whistle shatters the relative quiet of the platform. A look ahead and she is off to the capital city. The fireman looks back along the train, soon he will be swinging his shovel, a master of his trade.

His Midland counterpart will also bend his back many times before he reaches his destination, only the method will differ. Two Regions of one united body, British Railways yet so different in many ways. One small example of this is in the overalls that the enginemen wear. The Western men wear coat and trousers whilst the Midland crews wear the bib and brace type. Old traditions certainly die hard. Looking back I suppose that we Western fans used to knock the Midland supporters quite a bit. Their Barrow Road Shed was quite an outpost for their Region. Some people considered them as the poor relation in the area. We used to call them "Let Me Sleep" or "Lean, Mean and Sooty", we used to say that the Western had fireman, whilst the Midland had stokers.

Our unkind remarks would soon be forgotten after a visit to Fishponds Bank. To stand there and watch a 'Jubilee' or a 'Caprotti Five' in full cry was certainly a sight to capture the hearts of the most ardent Western followers. Another of our favourite pastimes was to travel by train from Bedminster to Temple Meads. Bedminster was our local station, its platforms were swept daily, during the summer months the flower beds were ablaze with colour. Bees winged their way happily amongst the variety of blooms whose scent filled the air. During the colder months, a roaring fire in the waiting room, welcomed travellers. Great pride was taken in the stations appearance.

A sizeable signal box situated at the end of the platforms controlled the 'up' and 'down' main, relief, avoiding lines as well as the goods connection to the Pylle Hill Yard. Signals were situated at either end of the station, plus a backing board situated on the road arch close to the Catholic School. The return fare to Temple Meads was two old pence, and for us young spotters the short journey held its own special delights. We would board either a Weston-Super-Mare stopper or a local off the Portishead Branch. Sometimes we would board an empty stock train from Malago Sidings which had been stopped at the signal gantry.

Shortly after our departure we would scan Victoria Park for any fellow spotters, waves would be exchanged. Our wave being somewhat superior, after all we were travelling in style. To our left we would explore Pylle Hill Goods Yard and catch a glimpse of the St. Philips Marsh based pilot engine going busily about its duties, a shunting gig rattling merrily behind. Sometimes we would see a transfer detaching some of its vans before proceeding to West Depot Yard. Our next passing point would be West Sidings, a coaching stock enthusiasts paradise. We were now under control by electric signalling from Bristol West Box. As we passed beneath the road bridge our eyes would be trained on the yard of Bath Road Shed. We would come to a halt on the appointed platform, disembark and devote the day to the study of the steam locomotive.

Activities on Sunday were few and far between and to spend a morning at Bedminster Station was a very different story when compared to the business of a weekday; traffic was light and the surrounding district was at rest. The hustle and the bustle of the local factories was missing. The bells from the many churches throughout the city could be heard calling their followers to their different places of worship. From the houses which backed on to the railway came the aroma of a Sunday lunch being prepared, the delicious smell of English beef and 'real' vegetables wafted through the air.

Such were my early impressions when every day was an adventure. So many changes have altered the railway scene in my local area, such changes are known as progress, but when I look back to the once busy stations, the numerous signal boxes and the amount of rail traffic that could be seen, these early memories become even more cherished to me.

Chapter 2

LEARNING THE TRADE

Two years after leaving school my dreams came true when I secured a position as an engine cleaner with British Railways Western Region.

Armed with enough cotton waste to do the job, and a packet of crushed brick dust in my overall pocket I left the St. Philips Marsh shed stores and went in search of 6876 *Kingsland Grange*. I found her gurgling quietly on the "large side roundhouse". The pile of cotton waste was put on her side framing, and the usual "NOT TO BE MOVED" target board was displayed on the front end. *Kingsland Grange* was still in British Railways unlined black livery, but she always polished up well.

I had just started to polish the copper band round her chimney when the

Chargehand appeared on the scene and dropped the bomb shell.

"A word in your ear Jim" was his opening sentence. I climbed down from my lofty perch and confronted him. "Next Monday you go on days for your firing test at Westbury".

Charming, I thought to myself, here I am just learning to become an engine cleaner, now they want me to become a Fireman. The necessary information relating to travelling etc, was passed on to me. We would book on at the 'Marsh', walk to Temple Meads and travel as passengers on the 8.5am Weymouth, but why Westbury? The last gathering of would-be firemen was instructed on their home ground. I continued with my cleaning with more than one thought inside my head.

The following Monday I booked on at the appointed time, and with my fellow cleaners made our way up to the station. Passing through Bath Road shed I noted 4507 residing there in green livery. Our train duly arrived, headed by a Bristol based 'Hall'. We settled down in our warm compartment, my fellow travellers consisting of three senior cleaners. They were, Rex Whitwam, a well built jovial fellow, from the country town of Keynsham, Terry Saunders, a local lad, and so relaxed rolling a cigarette and a Cornish lad from Bath Road who had seen service at Truro before moving to Bristol. They all had one thing in common - they had all gained experience with the firing shovel - I was the odd man out.

Our guardian angel and Instructor was Loco Inspector McCarthy, who was dressed in his usual attire, trilby hat, the brim turned down and a long sombre overcoat. A tall upright man with a wealth of information stored away inside his head that could be tapped at a moments notice.

Upon arrival at Westbury we followed "Mac", as he was affectionately known, down the short lane to the busy engine shed. Outside the stores we were met by the rest of our fellow pupils, we climbed the stairs to our classroom, which in fact was the room above the stores. Formalities were exchanged, it was then clear to me why Westbury had been chosen, for amongst the assembly of lads were three from Weymouth.

Seated around a long table with "Mac" at the head, our instruction on the noble art of firing began. First on the agenda was the preparation of a locomotive, "Mac" explaining that a good 'prep' was the keyword to becoming a good fireman. We went through the rule book over and over again, the rules were drummed into us so much so that after all these years most of them still come instantly to mind. Rule 55. Detention at Home or Starting signals; Rule 218 Obstruction of lines and protection, and rules 220 and 221 which covered engine failures, accidents, trains which had become divided. Question after question was fired at us, imaginary trains were laid out on the table, the engine and wagons were matchsticks, bent cigarette cartons were tunnels, some peculiar movements took place on the table with some matchsticks disappearing forever.

"Mac" kept on to us until we got it right, then he went on to pastures new and we started all over again, my mind was becoming a mass of figures numbers and regulations, would I ever remember it all? We learned all the various hand signals, which engines had flat grates, which ones had sloping grates, how to spot leaky tubes, and what to check inside the smokebox. During our short lunch break I would walk round the shed. Westbury was a Churchward built staight road shed consisting of four roads. An interesting array of locomotives could be seen, and it was nice to roam around without any questions being asked. There were a few examples of the auto fitted 54xx class on view, with their 5ft 2in wheels and tall chimnies, they became a favourite of mine.

63xx and 73xx Moguls were regular visitors, several of these being allocated to Westbury. In the yard was a 56xx 0-6-2T with a pair of her driving wheels missing. Several of this type were used regularly on the Upton Scudamore banker, and when we were in the classroom I would try to catch sight of the Radyr to Salisbury goods with a spotless 56xx or 66xx assisting an equally spotless 72xx up the bank. The sound of their combined efforts was music itself.

I noted a 2-8-2T 7225 from distant Llanelly on shed, and 2-6-2T 4158 from Wellington shed resplendant in British Railways lined green livery. I saw 2875 which was still lettered GWR and my notebook records 5542 in open store in the shed yard. Traffic from the area was intense with locomen coming and going at all hours, a railway hostel was situated adjacent to the station. Westbury's locomotive stud was kept in immaculate condition, wheels and frames were not overlooked and their brass and copper work fairly gleamed.

We would return home every evening on a Weymouth to Bristol train and return to our seat of learning each morning. As the first week progressed "Mac" started to ask us questions on the train, but I still found time to record Pannier 8737 as being the Bath pilot that week. Our learning progressed; we coupled up and uncoupled, we went through the rule book, over the 'prep' again. Verbally we built up the fire, filled the sand boxes with "Mac" saying that we must all have been rather hot after our ordeal, for no one mentioned taking their coats off.

It was now time to put theory into practice, and on the 6th and 7th day we were let loose on the locomotives. First of all we were shown the principle of the injectors. I did my bit on Bath Road 'Castle' 5057 *Earl Waldegrave*. Some of us found her exhaust injector a bit tricky, and my first attempt sent clouds of steam down the yard with nothing happening to the level of water in the boiler.

"Mac" found out what was due to go off the shed from the foreman, and I was given Mogul 5312 to prepare, our instructor allowing me plenty of time, but reminded me that the booked time for getting a tender engine ready was one hour. It was nice to get out of the classroom and get to grips with the job in hand. I climbed aboard and hung my coat up, and opened the firebox doors to find she had a fairly large tump of fire burning in the centre of the grate and 30lbs of steam showing on the clock, so the blower could be used. I went through the prep; push the fire over the 'box, get it burning vigorously, check the smokebox, fill the sandboxes, and build up an appropriate fire for this type of locomotive. Her dials and backplate were covered with a film of white ash so after getting the fire into shape I gave everything a wipe down. With the injector singing merrily away I washed the footplate down and gave the coal a good wetting.

With the oil bottles warming nicely on the tray and a good pressure on the clock I was at peace with the world. I was enjoying a 'roll up' when our instructor appeared in the Mogul's cab. He checked the fire, and pointed out a few holes which I filled in immediately. He took a good look round and turning to me he remarked

"Nice and clean Jim, we might as well finish the job".

With him acting as driver I released the handbrake and we eased 5312 up to the water column, her crew having now arrived on the scene. I soon found out that it was the month of December, for standing on the back of the tender with the 'bag' in, I was catching the full force of the icey wind that was blowing. At my call of 'Whoa' the water was turned off and the column was swung clear. I returned to the footplate to retrieve my coat.

"Bit parky today my dear" said the Westbury driver, "Try a little drop of this". He reached inside his bag and produced a small bottle and a tin mug. A drop of liquid was poured into the mug and passed my way. "Elderberry wine" he said "For medicinal purposes only". I left 5312 glowing both inside and out.

The next day we returned to the classroom for more tuition, and after dinner we were introduced briefly to the inside motion of 5402. Under instruction we were allowed to drive her up and down the yard, which gave me a great thrill. The last day of our fortnight's training dawned. More questions were asked on the train, with me getting about half of them right. After question time "Mac" travelled back in time telling us stories of 'Bulldogs' and 'Aberdares', naturally I was all ears. That final day we went through it all again, for the following day, Saturday we were to take our final test. "Mac" said we should be alright, but I did not share his confidence. We left the shed at the usual time to catch the 1.40pm ex-Weymouth home. I glanced back at the shed with the famous White Horse on the hill in the background. I had enjoyed my acquaintance with the busy depot.

Our train duly arrived, headed by a rather grubby 4969 *Shrugborough Hall*. "Mac" had a word with the driver and beckoned me to the engine.

"Up you go son" he said. I climbed aboard the 'Hall' with a feeling of great excitement. I was greeted by the Bath Road crew and a bit of good natured leg pulling was directed my way,

"Get your coat off mate" was the fireman's opening sentence, this remark was followed by a friendly wink. On the stroke of 3.28pm we got the right away, the bark from our 'Hall' was a thrilling sound to a young cleaner. I was as green as 4969's livery. I looked down the train just like the real fireman did.

"Right then mate, let's see what we can do" said the fireman.

The flap was lowered to reveal a mass of glowing fire dancing on the bars. Picking the shovel up I fired to his instruction, the driver had notched up and the familiar sounds of the GWR engine at work were all around me. The metalic ring of the shovel on the shoe, the rumble of the coal in the tender, the chatter of the fireirons, the steady beat of our two cylinder engine, familiar sounds to enginemen, but to me they were wildly exciting. The movement of our 'Hall' was also very noticeable with the cab swaying one way, the tender the other and the plate between them finding a happy medium.

We were booked to stop at Trowbridge, Bradford-on-Avon and Bath, between the stations I did my best with the shovel, the fireman shouting above the din that "little and often" was the name of the game, or "fire to the chimney". I tried my hand with both injectors, once again I found a little

The only existing photograph of the author at work on the footplate, acting as driver on the right, with Alan Hill on the shovel. Both were cleaners at the time, the locomotive being Mogul 5321, at St. Philips Marsh in 1958.   *(Author's collection)*

23

difficulty with the exhaust injector setting it against the groove, cut out in the bar, it blew out. After a minor adjustment I struck lucky. I was beginning to enjoy myself, the atmosphere was terrific, 4969 was in good nick and steamed quite freely.

Mile after mile went by, after Bradford the firing was eased, the fireman calling out all the signals and pointing out all the places of interest to me, we dropped down towards Bathampton with a piercing shriek on the whistle for the farm crossing, our 'Hall' was slowed down for the curve to join the main line. Stately Bath was reached, the fireman left the footplate to use the telephone on the post. With both signals showing clear we got the green flag and barked away from the Georgian masterpiece. The city was left behind us as we entered the castle like portal of Twerton tunnel. After 264 yards of darkness we passed beneath the main road and on to the long curving embankment to Saltford.

Just before the tunnel the fireman swung the heavy pricker bar down from the tender.

"Give her a pull round" he shouted. The bar was slid into the firebox and the doors closed just before we entered the musty smelling bore. Out into the daylight, the white hot pricker was removed and safely stowed away.

"That will get us home" said the fireman. "We've one more little job for you to do" he added. "We are going to pick up water from Foxes Wood troughs". He jammed the hand brush under the fall plate, unlocked the scoop and retired to the far corner of the cab. As we approached the troughs I noticed that the driver had put his feet upon the reverser.

I got the scoop down alright, but I was 'miles' too slow bringing it up - a large wave of water mixed with coal dust headed my way, followed by a roar of laughter from the crew. I picked up the handbrush and swept the slurry over the side hoping that "Mac" was not looking out of the window. We shot through St. Annes tunnel and at its exit the regulator was closed and we passed by the busy yards of East Depot.

With the city of Bristol spread out before us through the network of signals and points we went into Temple Meads station. A final touch on the brakes and we came to a rest in number 4 platform.

I put my coat on and said my farewell's to the crew and *Shrugborough Hall*. As I stepped down from the footplate the driver had the last word —

"Remember mate, the first ten years are the worst".

I walked down the platform like a ship rolling in a storm, my legs still reacting to the 'Halls' movements. I rejoined my mates and we headed for the 'Marsh' to book off, with more leg pulling to contend with.

The following day we returned to normal, 6am to 2pm working. At 9am I walked over the avoiding line bridge to meet "Mac" for my final test at Bath Road shed. Sat in the gloom of the cleaner's cabin "Mac" started his questions and my mind went blank, our instructor was not a hard man, so after a smoke we resumed the test. Thanks to his kindness I muddled through with him pronouncing me 'Passed'. I returned to the 'Marsh', and was ready to do battle with the Pilot Link.

It is said that things go full circle. Twenty one years later when collecting information for my first book I went to see retired driver Norman Anderson, I had heard his name mentioned many times over the years but I must admit that his face was new to me. After several hours of talking Norman said that he knew me, and as the evening went by his memory reached back through the mists of time.

"I've got it" he said. "Remember a nervous cleaner boy that fired a 49xx back from Westbury, well I was the driver that day".

Chapter 3

SUB SHED LIFE

The rumours concerning our future had been running wild. I had been employed as an engine cleaner at St. Philips Marsh and had taken my firing test at Westbury shed during 1957, where under the watchful eye of Inspector McCarthy I had been passed for firing. My grade was now known as a 'Passed Cleaner'. There was certainly an air of excitement as I walked into the cleaner's cabin that day and my mates were full of it. I wondered if anyone had stopped to think that soon our cleaning gang would be broken up and that we would be spread throughout the Bristol network. Some of us would travel even farther afield.

The familiar figure of our Chargehand, Bill Reed arrived on the scene, complete with his green beret perched aloft and he soon justified our fears (or delights). Bill handed out a pile of forms, one to each of us, informing us that we were to be made up to the rank of Fireman. We were instructed to give three choices of depot. At the top of my list I put St. Philips Marsh followed by Bath Road with my final choice being the Midland depot at Barrow Road. I felt sure that I had a good chance of staying at Bristol, (but the powers that be had other plans). After the paper work had been completed we were put to work, my job for that afternoon being the grooming 2-6-0 Mogul 6348. She was still in BR black livery, so as usual a mixture of cleaning and engine oil was applied to her. Standing on the handrail I started with her cast iron chimney working my way towards her cab. Dropping down to her running plate I then "blacked in" her bottom half. As I worked my thoughts began to wander,

25

Castle class 4-6-0, 4098 Kidwelly Castle in the yard at Bristol Bath Road on 19th August 1951. (D.H. Ballantyne)

perhaps one day I would fire old 6348 herself.

Several weeks later I was instructed to report to Bath Road shed. I was a little disappointed as my years at S.P.M. had been very happy. I had made some good mates whilst being in the 'number one' cleaning gang, but had to follow my destiny. On the appointed morning I made my presence known to the Bath Road Shed Foreman. He had quite a surprise in store for me. I was given a handful of free passes and told to report to the shed at Yatton. Yatton! The name rebounded around inside my head, I had passed the place many times on my journeys to Weston-Super-Mare and I had often seen the 14xx 0-4-2T with her two trailers standing in the bay platform, now I was going to work there.

The Foremans voice brought me back to the world of reality.

"I want you to go down and learn the auto son, so make your way up to the station, your train leaves in twenty minutes."

I left his office to carry out his instructions. As I waited for my train to arrive the butterflies in my stomach did a wild dance. What would it be like, would I be man enough to do the job? My train duly arrived hauled by a grubby 'Hall'. Station after station went by and with my deep thoughts occupying all the journey it passed very quickly and soon we were braking for Yatton Junction. I disembarked and crossed the main line by the way of the footbridge.

As I made my way down the platform the porter paused from his duties and stared at me, in fact his eyes stayed with me until I disappeared off the end of the platform. Perhaps it was the fourteen inch bottoms on my overalls trousers or was it the gold, black and blue striped shirt that I was wearing. For this was the "teddy boy" era and this apparition from the big city was interesting or perhaps a little amusing to a local railway man.

I made my way to the small engine shed which was empty except for the lone figure of the Shedman, going about his duties, I approached him.

"You must have come down to join us", he said.

My rather nervous answer received the usual look,

"Go down the station son, she is coming in soon".

I retraced my steps. From the end of the platform I took a look at the surrounding countryside. To my left the Chedder Valley line curved away, whilst to my right and the other side of the main line, the line to Clevedon curved away past the engine shed and beneath the road bridge. I had been used to a large engine shed and all the activity that went with it, all those green fields seemed very unfriendly to me.

My thoughts were suddenly disturbed by the squeal of flanges and I turned to watch 0-4-2T 1454 looking very spruce in British Railway's unlined green livery, propelling her two auto trailers into the bay platform. There was a hiss as the brakes were applied and she came to rest. Those butterflies in my stomach had now multiplied three fold. The passengers alighted from the train and the driver left his rear end driving compartment, I walked forward to meet him and to tell him that I had been sent down to 'learn the ropes'.

"Best come with me then mate" he replied, and we boarded the 14xx.

The pleasing aroma of steam and warm oil greeted us, as I was introduced to the fireman and after the usual formalities I stowed my bag in the corner of the cab and familiarised myself with the controls. The 14xx's were compact little machines but there was not much room on the footplate for three men. Our connecting train arrived, a few of its passengers boarding our auto. A whistle was blown and the train departed, her exhaust beats becoming fainter as she went beneath the road bridge; just the sound of 1454's safety valve disturbing the peace as the needle on the pressure gauge pushed hard against the 165lb mark. Our own departure time had now arrived, our road ahead was clear, the driver checked his watch, a look behind from the fireman, a toot on the whistle and we were off to Clevedon. We made our way past the loco shed and under the roadbridge. The smoke from our 'Fourteen's' tall chimney rebounded from the underside of the bridge and smothered the roofs of the following auto trailers. We ran out into the open countryside, there being no intermediate stations on this branch line.

The fireman handed me a shovel and asked me if I would "Like a go at her." He told me that she liked her four corners fed. There was plenty in her bowels so I just splashed a few around her. Our 'Fourteen' had been notched up and was purring along quite steadily at 30mph. I leaned out of the cab and soaked in the atmosphere. The green fields went by, cows and sheep grazed contentedly unconcerned at our approach. We passed under several overbridges one of which was quite unique in the fact that it had a post box built into its parapet. We rattled our way over a small bridge that spanned a stretch of water known as 'The Little River'.

The branch was a mere 3 miles 45 chains in length so it was time to close the regulator and apply the brakes as the terminus of Clevedon was reached. We came to a halt at seven minutes past nine, dead on time. The lady Station Mistress stood on the platform surveying the scene as our passengers detrained. Clevedon station had an overall roof and very lengthy platforms for a branch line station, with a goods yard on the right and a crossover road on the left.

Our driver left the footplate and walked to the end of the train. From the compartment there, he would drive the train. All the necessary controls were coupled from the engine through to the rear driving position. The ingenious auto, or push-and-pull design enabled single line working to be carried out without having to uncouple the engine and to run round the train at the start or finish point. At 9.10am we were ready to depart and would propel back to Yatton. The fireman sat down on the driver's seat, I banged a few around the

The tiny loco shed at Frome with two 0-6-0 Pannier tanks, including 3629 half in the shed.
(P. Nicholson collection)

box, lifted up the flap and put the injector on, I also took the opportunity to give the coal a good damp down in the bunker. The driver gave us one bell, the engine was put into back gear, the blower was opened a turn. A warning blast on the whistle and we departed for Yatton. It was a very strange feeling to be driven from the other end, but it was very nice to have more room on the footplate.

I was allowed two weeks training on auto working and was passed by Inspector McCarthy on a 55xx class 2-6-2T engine. There were several instructions to be learnt on this type of job. First of all there were the bell codes which were as follows, 1 ring to start; 2 rings for the fireman to blow brake off; 3 rings to stop. Other regulations were:- where guards were not employed on auto trains the following applied:

1) The Station Master or other authorised person must see that the tail lamp is in position and burning properly when necessary before the train leaves the starting point.

2) The signal for starting will be given by the Station Master or other authorised person.

3) In the event of the train being stopped by accident or other exceptional causes the driver must satisfy himself that all is in order before proceeding again with the train.

4) In the event of an accident, or failure of the train, the train must be considered as coming within the category of a light engine. It goes without saying that there had to be complete understanding between driver and fireman, especially when propelling.

Two of our own instructions which had to be obeyed were that when

29

running into the bay platform at Yatton the fireman would assist the driver by applying the handbrake and that the locomotive be stopped with her gangway opposite the two corresponding lines painted on the station wall. This being the ideal place for a 14xx to take water from the column. Now that I had been passed for auto working I would be linked with a regular driver. Our first meeting was a disaster, infact the first of a line of disasters. On the appointed day I walked into the tiny cabin at Yatton, there sat my mate. He took one look at me and virtually erupted.

First of all I was told that I was too young to do this type of work, that I should be in the Pilot Link in Bristol and that I had no business being at Yatton. He proclaimed that he would get in touch with Bath Road and demand that an older hand be sent down. He shuffled out of the shed towards the station, with me a good two yards behind him. Things became impossible, the more I tried to please him the worse the situation became. I began to dread going to work—only my love of railways kept me going.

We had two early turns at Yatton; 3.15 and 4.15am. This in itself caused a considerable problem for yours truly. The last train from Bristol that stopped at Yatton was the 10.30pm, and when I caught this train I was faced with a long cold wait in the engine shed or the station waiting room. On one occasion I made my own way there, but not through choice.

I had attended a wedding reception and overstayed, thus missing my train. There was only one thing for it, out came my trusty old push bike, off I set well after midnight with just the friendly beam from my headlamp to keep me company. It was very chilly and the roads were very quiet. I was cycling quite merrily through Long Ashton when I was stopped and surrounded by four very tall gentlemen wearing long overcoats, one of them produced his identification, they were plain clothes detectives. They had been watching my approach from a parked car discreetly hidden up a side road. I was asked where I was going at this unearthly hour. When I told them that I was going to work they just stood there with their mouths open. A look of utter disbelief and amazement on their faces!

After quite a bit of explaining they began to believe me, especially after searching my bag which held a tea can and sandwiches. After a few choice phrases such as "The best of luck mate" and "You must be mad", I set off once more. The farther afield I cycled, the quieter it became. I passed through sleeping villages, their church towers standing guard over their slumbering parishes like grey sentinels in the darkness. Eventually I reached the junction road for Yatton after much huffing and puffing. The main road had been very quiet and the side road I had just entered was like a mortuary. The silence was occasionally broken by scuttling sounds from the hedgerow as an animal went on its nightly search for food. Then something happened that really made my heart skip a beat.

Suddenly a huge head appeared over a gateway, there was a flash of eyes, and a cloud of steaming breath from the monster's nostrils. A huge bellow pierced the silence. If someone would have been standing on that spot with a stopwatch a few cycling records would have been broken. My legs worked overtime, the wheels flew round in an effort to get away from this fearsome intruder. I reached the end of the road where I stopped to regain my breath. After my racing pulse had slowed down I cautiously looked back to the gateway, there looking at me with a somewhat old fashioned look on her face was the 'monster'—a friendly old cow.

Eventually my destination was reached, I parked my steed and got on with the job in hand of preparing the 14xx for the coming day. As the warmth from the fire slowly enveloped the cab I forgot the chill and saddle-soreness. I had plenty of time in hand, so after completing my own duties I turned my attention to the oiling up. Armed with a flare lamp and a feeder I dropped into the pit and took care of things beneath the 14xx. As I emerged from the pit my mate arrived on the scene and I told him that all was in order. He looked at me and grunted: I thought of the journey that I had taken to get there, all my driver had to do was travel a short distance. The day was like any other, I was told that I should be working in Bristol, that I lacked experience. I replied that I did not ask to come to Yatton, peace reigned once more and did so for the next eight hours.

On the morning duty we used to pick up several box vans from the goods yard at Clevedon. These were loaded with confectionary from the local cake factory. We would attach these vans to the front of the engine and with us sandwiched in the middle we would propel both goods and passengers back to Yatton. We were also called upon to take part in shunting activities. One such duty was the handling of traffic from the Caperns bird seed factory.

My favourite turn of duty was the late one. The last train departing from Clevedon somewhere in the region of 10.33pm. The Salthouse was and still is a very popular public house. Many of its patrons travelling by rail. The courting couples would say their goodnights in the dark corners of the station, a toot on the whistle would bring them running to board the train. On more than one occasion several members of the fairer sex had asked me if they could ride back on the footplate. I never refused them but made it quite clear that as soon as we reached Yatton they would have to get off the engine a 'bit quick'. The less my mate saw the better.

The first thing that these stowaways had to watch was their stilleto heels in the cracks in the wooden floorboards, great care was also taken that their stockings did not come into contact with various metal objects bolted to the cab of a 14xx class. My rewards for letting these trespassers ride with me varied; tabacco, crisps, and an occasional bottle of brown ale being the main rewards. Upon reaching Yatton the ladies would beat a hasty retreat and my mate would be none the wiser. Such feminine aromas as perfume would be swallowed up by the natural smells of the steam engine and not a clue remained, until one Saturday night. My "passengers" had disembarked and all was quiet on the footplate. My driver had left his rear end compartment and had climbed aboard, he glared at me then asked if I was expecting rain. I was puzzled, then I saw it hanging on the whistle chain — a bright red umbrella! My trips with the joy riders were over.

During my time at Yatton my mind had been in a turmoil. I had tried to transfer back to Bristol, but to no avail. One afternoon my mate went sick. Bath Road sent down a passed fireman to fill in his absence. That afternoon was a real treat for me. I confided in him and he came up with a good suggestion. Why not transfer to another department? This would be a good way of getting back to Bristol and I could also stay a railway servant. After a great deal of thought I went through the necessary channels. On my next rest day I had an interview with Inspector Alex James in the old part of Temple Meads station, he was one of the heads in charge of the Signalling Department in the Bristol area. Eventually my transfer went through and a date was set.

Life at Yatton continued until one day on the Cheddar things came to a head. An almighty row started which ended with me giving the shovel to my mate and telling him what he could do with No.41202 the engine in question. Talk about a transformation. He apologised and offered me the regulator and he took charge of the firing. Unfortunately his change of heart had come too late. It was not long before my last days there came around, this final period was to become a mixture of both sadness and joy. My transfer would mean that I would be closer to home, and I would not have to face those early morning bike rides. On the Friday night we put 1454 on shed and I said my farewells to my driver. He shook hands with me and wished me well. Deep down he was not a bad sort of chap. We went our different ways, I made my way to the station and at the foot of the platform I stopped to take a last look. The peace of the countryside was disturbed only by the chorus of late birds and the far off gurgles from the 14xx. A part of my life was about to end.

Such was life at Yatton, be it good or bad. The little stone shed at Yatton closed its doors to business in August 1960.

I mentioned in chapter one that my first view of Bath Road shed was from the top of a bus. It was from this vantage point that I was also to witness the end of an era. I remember that day in 1960 quite vividly. Standing on the stores road that day were Nos 1412 and 1454 coupled together. Their destination was Swindon Works. 1412 the leading engine was blowing off furiously at the safety valves as if to say "I've got plenty of life left in me". Her protesting was in vain. I was witnessing the end of the auto train in my local area.

Regarding the 14xxs associated with Yatton, the following come to mind.

One of the two station pilots employed at Temple Meads during the steam era 0-4-2T 1454 in BR unlined green livery on West Sidings pilot duty, 3rd June 1957. (Author)

My earliest memories recall Nos 1415 and 1430. Other regulars were 1409 and 1463 and as mentioned 1412 and 1454. 1412 was reallocated from Oswestry, she was still in GWR green livery whilst 1454 came from Weymouth at about the same time. During 1959 1409 became surplus to requirements after spending several weeks on the St. Philips Marsh large side roundhouse. She was dispatched light engine to Gloucester, being withdrawn from that division in October 1963. 1463 was withdrawn in April 1961 also from Gloucester. Both she and 1409 had one thing in common. They were both finished in BR black livery but someone had stripped the paint from their safety valves covers revealing the brass finish. Someone must have really loved those two little engines. No. 1415 was withdrawn in February 1957 from Southall; 1430 was withdrawn from Gloucester in September 1958, this being the home of perhaps one of the most famous auto trains, the Chalford car. During 1957 No. 5403 was reallocated to Bath Road from Westbury, but was withdrawn the following August. A 64xx 0-6-0 Pannier tank made a brief appearance on Clevedon auto in 1959. We called her the "square banger" because anything that could rattle on her did. (My notes have not recorded her number).

During BR days Bath Road or St. Philips Marsh supplied a Pannier tank to the sub shed at Bath for use on the pilot duties there, this small depot having its busy times during earlier years. At one time two sets of men were employed on the pilot. The first set booked on duty at 5.15am and prepared the engine which went off shed at 6am. Those early men were relieved at 1pm by the second set who worked through to 9pm the engine then returning to shed.

Pilot work at Bath included the stabling of any coaches which were "slipped" there, one of these was from a 'Down' London. On two mornings of the week the early morning pilot came on duty at 5am to shunt the wagons for the Acton meat train. The West Moreland Yard also had to be shunted. This yard handled coal and the movement of crane parts from Messrs. Stothert and Pitt a local heavy engineering company. These parts were brought into the yard by their own fleet of Foden steam lorries, an Inspector being sent down from Swindon to examine any out of gauge loads that sometimes occurred.

During the nineteen twenties the celebrated Bath and West Show was held at the Georgian city. This occasion created a great deal of extra traffic which sometimes required an extra engine being sent out from Bristol. Another busy period was the racing season, a large amount of horse box traffic being handled for the Lansdown race course. If a shortage of men occurred a senior driver would be sent by Bristol. The afternoon pilot would shunt the West Moreland Yard as and when required and would position the coal empties for the Chippenham goods and the "Didcot Fly". The pilot would then shunt on the upside until 7pm (depending on the traffic) her final duty of the day would be to go to the top yard and get the London traffic ready. During the twenties the outside crank panniers were used on the pilot, No. 1149 being one of these. During the later years the 77xx class were the usual engines. Nos. 3731, 7749 and 8737 being three contenders, all from St. Philips Marsh shed.

Another duty the pilot took care of was the supply of coal to the Bath Electric Light Company. Generally six wagons at a time being the usual load. Upon arrival at this siding one wagon at a time would be detached and turned to the private siding by way of a small turntable. From here another "pilot" would take over, a four legged variety, a sturdy horse. This four legged shunter sometimes used to move horse boxes to and from the fishdock.

During the 'steam car' era five sets of men were stationed at Bath. The rail cars put in some sterling work and were used extensively over many routes, two of the Bath based steam car duties were as follows; all stations from Bath to Bristol then all stations to Pilning Low Level. Departing from there at 8.15am the car then ran on service to Portishead calling at all stations en route. Departing from Portishead at 9.40am the car returned to Bristol leaving there for Calne 12.25am the crew having relief at Bath. For this lengthy duty sacks of coal were stacked around the cars vertical boiler. Another busy day began with booking on and travelling to Bristol as passengers on a 'Down' Reading train. After walking to St. Philips Marsh shed the men would take to a rail car and work from Temple Meads to Calne, then return to Chippenham and Trowbridge. Departing from there at 5.20pm the car and its trailer returned to Chippenham waiting there for the 4.30pm ex London, this train detaching a slip coach at Chippenham.

The staff at Bath take a break and pose for the camera, with Fireman J. Gullis and his driver, smiling from the cab of an outside crank pannier tank. (Author's collection)

This coach was attached to the car's trailer and the complete train departed at 6.20pm, all stations to Bath. Upon arrival the now empty coach would be stabled in the middle road, the trailer in the bay and the car would go on shed. The demise of the versatile steam cars brought much regret to the men that knew them, but to progress it was just another closing chapter in our railway's history.

The healing waters of Bath Spa are nationally known and the GWR station was equipped for handling visitors of an infirmed nature. On the downside a pumping station was situated which operated the hydraulic lifts which catered for passenger's wheel chairs and the like. Sunday duties at Bath included engineering trains in the Box Tunnel. Life at Bath shed expired in the early sixties.

The single road shed at Weston-Super-Mare was opened in 1861 by the Bristol and Exeter railway. Pre war duties from this shed included the 4.35pm passenger train to Westbury, a duty to Swindon and a milk train to Taunton which was generally rostered to one of the depots 'Bulldog'' class engines. During later times the following duties were covered by Weston men. The pick-up goods engine went off shed at 4am, the men booked on at 3.15am and preparing the 77xx class engine. The 'Up' journey included a shunt at the Puxton and Worle dairy, wagons were also put off and collected from Yatton Junction, West Depot and St. Philips Marsh goods. The train returned from here calling at West Depot (once again), Flax Bourton, Yatton, Nailsea and Puxton and Worle, the remaining wagons being put away upon arrival at Weston. Because of the importance of the route taken, the train was held up in the various yards and loops for lengthy periods, making the job a rather lengthy operation, with twelve hours on duty not being unusual. During earlier times a standard goods class being the rostered engine.

The passenger duties were the 6.30am Cardiff which called at all stations. First to Severn Tunnel Junction, followed by a stop at Newport. At Cardiff the empty stock was put away and the engine went on Canton shed for coal and water. The balance duty from Cardiff General was to Portsmouth which was worked forward by Weston men to Bath. During the Second World War period it was a very heavy train consisting of 13 packed coaches at times. On occasions a two cylinder 63xx class was rostered to the job and with such a heavy load behind her tender a banker was put on at Severn Tunnel Juction for assistance through the tunnel and over Patchway bank. During later years the duty was revised with Weston men having relief at Stapleton Road.

There was the 6am which ran to Filton, whilst another duty involved the preparation of four locomotives. A rough days work was one of the depots Sunday turns. This started with the 1.30pm to Bristol, where upon arrival the engine was taken off and turned at Bath Road Shed, also going under the tip there to take coal and water from the column. The engine then returned with the 3.50pm ex Bristol to Weston, where once again she came off and turned, returning to Bristol with the 6.45pm to London. Another turn around at Bath Road was undertaken before returning to Weston with the 8.45pm. The engine being turned for the fifth and final time at Locking Road.

A pilot engine was kept at Weston, one of her duties being the movement of wagons to and from the gasworks. This involved a shunt being made across the road under the protection of the shunter who was also responsible for the controlling of the road traffic. The GWR engine was not allowed inside the gasworks, their own locomotive which was capable of hauling three wagons at a time taking care of things within the confines of the gasworks, which when at full output could stable as many as eighty wagons.

Weston-Super-Mare is well known as a popular seaside resort and during the summer season it took on an air of feverish activity. At the commencement of each summer service the pilot would completely clear the yard and the various sidings of all stock. These would be stabled at Uphill, Worle Junction and Brent Knoll. During peak periods as many as one hundred engines per day could be found either passing through, turning or stabling there. Locking Road station was one of the top revenue earners on the GWR network, but when economy reared its ugly head this did not stop Dr. Beeching from closing it.

Other passenger duties were the 1.45pm to Bristol, take coal and water from Bath Road, run to Malago Vale, pick up the empty stock and work a train through to Severn Beach and Pilning. Another good days work was the 11.33am Weston to Exeter which ran on a Sunday. Upon arrival the engine was turned and coaled on Exeter shed. She then ran attached to another engine and train to Taunton, where the Weston engine came off and waited in the bay platform. At the appropriate time this engine worked a passenger duty forward to Bristol returning to Weston with a similar train.

During the Second World War period an American ambulance train was stabled on the number four platform road at Locking Road station. This train was kept in a state of readiness enabling it to be moved at a moments notice. During the winter an engine was kept on this train for steam heating purposes. During the latter days of steam, Weston men worked the 12.15am to Bristol and walked from Temple Meads to Barrow Road shed to prepare an engine.

Diesel traction appeared at Weston in the early Sixties ousting the small steam allocation. A 350 hp shunter taking over the pilot duties and the DMUs looking after the passenger traffic. The remaining four drivers having gone to Swindon to learn the new traction. The little shed finally closed its doors in November 1968, the existing men being offered jobs at such distant places as Southall, Reading and Whitland in West Wales.

The last link in the sub shed chain was Wells. The depot was opened in 1879 and had two roads with the normal allocation consisting of two locomotives. Once again both Bath Road and St. Philips Marsh supplying engines. During later years the versatile 55xx class covered the passenger duties whilst a standard goods of a 22xx 0-6-0 took care of the goods traffic.

From 1959 Wells man worked the following duties. On duty 5.55am for the 7.10am Wells to Yatton passenger returning with 11.10am Yatton to Witham, returning to Wells with 1.30pm, have relief, book off duty 2.25pm. The men for the afternoon passenger booked on at 1.50pm for the 2.00 Wells to Bristol, where upon arrival the engine went on Bath Road shed for coal. This was followed by the engine working the 6.5pm forward to Weston-Super-Mare, returning from there as light engine to Yatton for the 8.49pm to Wells. During 1959 this duty was taken off during the week and ran Saturdays only.

The goods duties were as follows. The 8.55am Bristol which did shunting at Wookey Hole Paper Mill and a great deal of Cheddar stone was carried on this train, Batscombe Quarry supplying a large amount of ballast to BR during the steam era. The Wells men changing footplates with Bristol men on the 'Down' goods at Axbridge. The other goods turn being the 8.40am Wells to Witham, the locomotive on this job also shunting at Dulcote Quarry, Shepton Mallet, Cranmore and Witham. It was here that the train was relieved by a set of Westbury men.

By 1961 the duties of Wells had dwindled down to two, these being the 7.10am Wells to Yatton passenger and the 1.55pm Wells to Cheddar goods for stone traffic. The Ivatt Moguls had by now become regulars over the branch on the goods traffic, 46525 being one of the chief contenders. The shed closed in November 1963, the four footplate men being transferred to Bath Road, all passenger traffic ceasing to run shortly after this. One goods train continued to run for about six months before the end came.

Chapter 4

BRANCH LINE SERVICES

The Number Four, Five and Workmans link covered a wide variety of work over the various branch lines in the Bristol area. This chapter deals with some of these duties and generally describes some of the routes encountered. The period covered is the forties and fifties.

Without doubt one of the most scenic routes locally is the Portishead branch. Opened in 1867 by the Bristol and Portishead Pier and Railway Company as a broad gauge line it was eventually operated by the Bristol and Exeter Railway, before passing into GWR ownership. 'Down' trains generally departed from the old number eleven platform at Temple Meads. A ground frame operated by the shunter enabled locomotives to run around their trains under his directions. According to the 1947 timetable the first 'down' train departed at 5.27am and was listed as being third class, limited accommodation only. Ashton Gate, Ham Green, and Portbury were not called at by this service. The first all-stations train departed at 7am.

A description of the route in the steam era begins on the main line at Bedminster, the first stop after departure. This was a four platform station with two waiting rooms, ticket and parcels office and a small siding which served the local coal merchants. Any shunting here was carried out by the Pylle Hill goods pilot. The next passing point is Malago Vale carriage sidings which has both east and west exits, beyond this and beneath the roadbridge Parson Street station is situated. To the west of this the branch junction diverges from the main line. Trains running on either 'Down' main or 'Down' relief could be signalled across by the junction signal box.

With the busy yards of West Depot to the left Ashton bank is descended, whilst to the right of the line is Ashton Gate, the home of Bristol City Football Club. To the left, the large sawmills dominate the scene, and the loop line which forms the one side of the triangle with the main line. Many believe this to be a goods only loop, this was not so. The Portishead — Weston-Super-Mare Sunday school excursions used this route and it was not unusual to see a 55xx class at the head of ten coaches coming this way.

Ashton Crossing is passed, a blast on the whistle for the S.W. board here. At

Prairie tank 5574 in the Bath Road loco yard in 1958. This was one of the class fitted for auto train working and gave sterling service on the Clifton and Workman's Link. *(Author)*

the foot of the bank a left hand curve takes us into Ashton Junction. The signal box here controls the level crossing, sidings, loops and the entrance to the branch, the yard and the Bristol City Docks. One siding behind the signal box connected to the local steelworks. Beneath the road bridge the line diverged, Ashton Meadows Yard went off to the right, and a board here reminded enginemen that members of the 28xx, 42xx and 52xx classes were banned from certain roads. A similar board stated the 47xx class 2-8-0's were banned entirely. Running alongside the yard are the Bristol Harbour lines, these diverge once again at Avon Crescent signal box, where they go their separate ways to Cannons Marsh and Wapping Yard. The pilots and transfers of St. Philips Marsh shed were regular users of this route.

Directly ahead is the actual start of the branch and also the first station — Ashton Gate. During home matches at the nearby football ground this station became a scene of feverish activity. The many exits and the large footbridge helping to disperse the large crowds at the better attended matches. It was not unusual to see larger engines here at the head of football excursions. From here the line passes beneath a stone built bridge and climbs with a right hand curve up to Clifton Bridge Station. Coaching stock was stabled here in the loop and the refuge road. The local gangers cottage was also situated nearby. Clifton Bridge was where the first staff was picked up (Clifton Bridge to Oakwood).

39

From here the line continues to climb, curving right and then left towards the first tunnel, Clifton Bridge Number One. It is brick lined throughout and has a generous bore, a reminder of the broad gauge era. Directly above the tunnel is Brunel's graceful masterpiece, the Clifton Suspension Bridge. The rugged beauty of the Avon Gorge can now be enjoyed. Climbing above and to the left of the line is the torturous Rownham Hill which must have proved to be a nightmare for those early motoring pioneers. Below this the density of greeness begins. This is the start of the beautiful Leigh Woods, mile after mile of trees, wild flowers, and plant life.

The woods are a veritable blaze of colour, especially during the warmer months, various shades of green blend with the browns and silvers of the birches, trees of many species act as host to masses of ivy and various types of creepers. Large bunches of ferns line the lower banks. Brambles intermingle with the shrubbery twisting this way and that. In some parts of the woods the thickness of growth has formed a ceiling of green, so dense that the sun cannot penetrate it. The smell of damp earth fills the air encouraging the growth of mushrooms and fungi. Man too has made his mark amongst the plant life. This is in the form of round posts that mark the boundary of the GWR.

Large moss covered stones lay at intervals along the lineside. Dead trees lay choked and forgotten among the undergrowth whilst young saplings struggle for life amonst the damp soil. Evening time will find large swarms of gnats buzzing busily beneath the trees. To the right of the line at a lower level is the old tow path and beyond that the muddy River Avon winds her way down to the Channel. This is the river that made the Port of Bristol world famous. It was through these waters that Brunel's famous ship the *Great Britain* made her maiden voyage. During later years the graceful steamers of P.& A. Campbell were familiar sights along this stretch of water. The 'Glens' and the 'Queens' which gave so many generations pleasure could all be seen churning through the muddy waters with their revolving paddles.

The opposite bank of the river also had its points of interest. There was the Clifton Rocks Railway which was operated by the Bristol Tramways and Carriage Co. Ltd. Where in bygone days for a fare of one old penny passengers could ride to the top of Durdham Down. A very pleasurable spot during the summer, also situated on the opposite bank was the site of the old Bristol Port and Pier Railways Hotwells Station. This was demolished in 1922 to make way for the new road, The Portway.

We leave the suspension bridge behind us but we stay with woodland scenery. The line passes over the first bridge, the archway of this is the entrance to Nightingale Valley, a local beauty spot. The path through the valley climbs up sharply from the railway. From this area the pleasing aroma of woodsmoke often filled the air. This came from the couple of tin shacks situated close to the lineside. These were the homes of some less fortunate squatters. Still following the course of the river the Clifton Bridge Number Two Tunnel is reached. (232 yards in length.) Its rocky entrance shows the chisel marks of the navvies whose sweat and toil built the line. These men made impressions that will be their lasting testimony. Keeping in character with the curving route the tunnel has a bend in its middle. Above the tunnel exit is a smooth sloping slab of rock, this is known locally as the "Donkey Slider". For many years one single slogan adorned its face, which read 'Yanks go home', a plea from an unknown artist during the Second World War period. Several old quarry workings are passed, many years ago stone was carried away by barges, now bushes and small trees have made the rocky faces their home. The line now takes a further uphill grade and continues to curve with each bend of the river. Through the trees on the edge of the towpath the white painted navigation lights appear and disappear, guiding ships through the twisting Avon. Just beyond the 123¼ mileage post the mouth of Sandstone Tunnel is reached, which has a bore 88 yards in length. Beyond the tunnel the branch crosses an elegant looking four arch bridge. This is an interesting piece of engineering, for burrowing beneath the river bank is a tunnel which connects to a small basin fed by a woodland stream by way of a delightful waterfall. The tunnel is another reminder of the stone barge era. From the other side of the river this gives one the impression that there is a bridge with a smaller bridge beneath it.

The density of woodland scenery continues with interruptions at intervals by rocky walls. Winding paths disappear into the bracken leading to hidden valleys and leafy dales, wildlife abounds amongst the greenery. The line starts to curve inland away from the notorious Horseshoe Bend, which in bygone days was to be the death of quite a few vessels. The climb now stiffens and situated almost at the top of the bank is Oakwood Signal Box and passing loop. This is where the staff was changed. This box must have been a rather windswept place during the winter and quite a lonely place for the signalmen to attend. At the top of the bank is the 124¼ mile post.

Just beyond this in the cutting a towering three arch overbridge is passed and almost immediately the line takes a falling grade towards the next station. Situated on a right hand curve is Ham Green Halt. Its wooden platform on the 'Down' side is quite lengthy for a halt, a stone built extension having been added to this in later years. This halt dealt with a great deal of traffic for the nearby hospital, the nurses of which alighted there after a "night out" in Bristol, and are remembered by locomen as being a rather cheery bunch. Opposite the station is a peaceful stretch of water which almost reaches the line. This was known by railway staff as "Cripple Creek".

A short distance after the end of the platforms, on the right hand curve is Pill Tunnel. This is the longest bore on the branch being 665 yards in length. It was a very damp and smokey place. Situated near its exit is a soot encrusted

125¼ m.p. Some of the hospital wards are built above the tunnel, thus explaining those rumbles from deep in the ground many patients have experienced. Shortly after leaving the tunnel the Pill fixed distant is passed which is followed by the six arch Pill Viaduct. Below this is the small harbour and from the slipway at its entrance the Pill Ferry operated.

Believed to be one of the oldest ferries which operated in this country it has often been a friend to railway travellers. For many years it had been a family concern, the owners during the 19th century being a Mr. Porter and his wife Hannah. She would sit at the window of the old watch house with a pin cushion and a packet of pins. She would watch the passengers get on and off the ferry, and for everyone she would put a pin in the cushion. Come the end of the day she would check her tally with the money taken. Charles Porter died of a stroke in his own ferry boat. A family which was responsible for the service in later years was the Rice family. Tragedy also struck them when Jim Rice was drowned on a bitter cold day in December 1950. He slipped on the icy slipway and was swept away by the fast and treacherous Avon tide. The ferry operated from 5.40am to 10.40pm, and by 6am the whole slipway would be filled by a line of silent men most of them with bicycles on their shoulders waiting to go up the plank to board the waiting boat. Some of these men had beer for breakfast, the backdoor of the Swan Public House being kept unlocked for such early callers.

Many times the only connection with Bristol and Avonmouth has been the ferry. Overnight snow often closed the hill out of the village and even stopped the trains. For one week in 1964 the ferry was the only vital link.

Beyond the viaduct was Pill station (Crewkerne Pill or Crokerne Pill is the proper name of the village). The station was situated in a cutting with the houses and the inevitable Railway Inn above it. The station had two lengthy platforms, a passing loop, a signal Box (Downside) and a small goods yard. The Oakwood - Pill staff was set down. After leaving the station and curving further inland the branch reverts once again to single line. At Portbury Shipyard Signal Box, which also has a passing loop and three overgrown, rusting sidings, the staff is changed for the final time.

The next station which is Portbury had one platform on the left (Downside) and one siding. Beyond the roadbridge is the 128 mileage post which is followed by a straight run. Our destination can now be clearly seen. The chimnies of the power staiton reach to the sky like giant fingers, the cranes in the dockyard swing busily about their duties. The Gasworks Crossing is passed and the terminus of Portishead is reached by way of a sweeping right hand curve. The station here was double tracked, there were two platforms with a water column situated on the 'Up' one.

The refreshment room here, which is still remembered with affection, was unique. It was privately owned and a very nice pint of beer was served - just the tonic for a fireman's dry throat on a hot summers day! The station staff were a rather amiable bunch of men, the porters room was always welcome to a footplate man. Other installations included a single road engine shed, a turntable which was fitted with ramps for the Standard Goods Class that often used the branch, and an assortment of sidings, two of which stabled the Vobster Stone and Black Rock Quarry wagons. One of the "bobbies" in the local signal box was known as "the toff" because of his smart appearance which included a top hat and a freshly picked flower pinned to his jacket.

Beyond the station was a mill and beyond that closer to the water's edge was an old rotting wooden platform, an inheritance from the old Bristol and Portishead Pier Railway no doubt. The Weston, Clevedon and Portishead Light Railway had its own station close to the GWR, a siding of 22 chains connecting the two. Their rustic looking station was often described as being a "garden summer house with platforms". The "old" GWR station as it became known later closed in 1954. Trains then used the brand new station which had been erected closer to the town. It was very spacious with lengthy platforms and a large canopy. These modern surroundings certainly lacked the old world charm that the former station had to offer. A large yard was laid out nearby for the C.E.G.B. traffic.

The St. Philips Marsh—Radstock link worked the coal trains over the branch, supplying fuel to the Portishead Power Station. Their "A" station was constructed in 1926 and work commenced on the "B" station in 1949. The last eight coal burning boilers were converted to oil burning between 1971—4 with the last coal train running over the branch in 1974. Goods engines generally worked bunker first to Portishead and chimney first towards Bristol. There was no standard practice with the passenger locomotives, engines working either way, in both directions. The speed restriction over the branch was 40 mph.

During the summer months duties were a most pleasurable occupation, but with the coming of winter came the icy wind that would whip off the river and whistle down the gorge making it a most unfriendly place for both man and locomotive alike. The line through the wooded section would become covered with a carpet of leaves giving drivers a few anxious moments when restarting on the climb from Clifton Bridge Station. For many years members of the popular 55xx 2-6-2 tank class were the regulars on the branch passenger trains. During the mid 1950's there were twenty of these residing at Bath Road:- 5506, 5511, 5512, 5514, 5523, 5527, 5528, 5535, 5536, 5539, 5546, 5547, 5548, 5553, 5555, 5558, 5559, 5561, 5564, and 5572. The depot's 45xx class locomotives were also used over the branch. The members of the 4500—74 series being less popular because of their smaller water capacity—only 1000 gallons compared with 1300 gallons.

As a matter of interest, some of the allocation movements of these two classes to Bath Road Shed included - 4524 from Laira Nov. 1955. 4567 from Worcester, April 1957, and 4589 which had a very busy year in 1958. In January she moved from Truro to Treherbert, February found her at Bath Road, by June she was at Tondu and by October she had moved once again to Exeter. 5565 was at Yeovil before coming to Bristol. 5528 was the first of her class to be painted in British Railways green livery and 5532 was also thus treated in July 1957.

The engine that worked the last 'Down' passenger of the day left the coaches at Portishead and then returned light to Bath Road. She had been out at work all day and by the time she had been screwed down on the coal road her fire was blue with clinker and there was not much more than coal dust left in her bunker. The first 'Down' goods in the morning returned with the first 'Up' passenger of the day. The versatile 55xxs could be found on branch line passenger, workman's train, pilot duties and local stopping passenger trains. They were good revenue earners and were flogged quite unmercifully over some of the steeply graded routes. By the time they were ready for a visit to the shops they were often in a sorry state. When running with full tanks their footplates would become awash with water caused by numerous leaks. The joint beneath the tank gauge also showing signs of wear by spraying water on all and sundry. Of course as the water level dropped these discomforts receeded.

The branch line coaching stock was supplied by Dr. Days sidings. The return fare from Paddington to Portishead in 1947 was twenty two shillings and ninepence third class. Going back to 1912 my mother can remember travelling from Bedminster to Portishead on the workman's train for six old pence return. An assortment of locomotives were used over the route on both goods and passenger duties including 17xx, 20xx, 36xx, 77xx, 87xx 0-6-0 Pannier tanks; 84xx, 94xx taper boilered 0-6-0 Pannier tanks; Standard Goods 2301 class; BR Standard class 3MT 82xxx series. 2-6-2 tanks and the GWR railcars were also regular visitors. Towards the end of the steam era, Barrow Road men worked over the branch with the 82xxx class with Western drivers acting as pilotmen on occasions. During the final years the DMU's took care of things, steam acting as a substitute when required.

The passenger service was withdrawn on 7th September 1964, much to the disappointment of the local community. As for the branch today the track is intact throughout, although some of the sleepers are in a sorry state. The station platforms can still be seen, but the buildings and the signal boxes have been demolished and the passing loops lifted. The line is now used as required by the occasional cement train. My recent quest for information took me along the route as far as Pill, and standing in the tranquility of the woods that day it was not difficult to 'hear' the sharp bark of a 55xx class once again.

As a postscript to the Portishead Branch I must mention that the once

Pannier tank 9453 at Temple Meads, 4th August 1952 on a service to Avonmouth and Severn Beach, following attention from the cleaning gang. (R.W. Hinton)

popular Pill ferry is also a memory. The new Avonmouth bridge which takes the motorway over the River Avon put the final nail in its coffin, the service coming to an end on 1st October 1974. No more will the once familiar cry of "last boat" be heard as the ferryman turned up his collar against the elements to take his final customers of the day safely home to Shirehampton.

Another service of great importance and one time good revenue earning, was the Avonmouth branch. Actually two routes can be taken, one diverged from the main line at Ashley Hill Junction whilst the other branched off at Filton Junction. The three Bristol sheds were involved in the activities over these routes, the Midland joining the GWR at Narroways Junction. In bygone years they once operated a passenger service from Clifton Down to Mangotsfield and Fishponds. Once again the Bath Road Number Five and workmans Link was involved in the operating of these routes.

During the late forties the first train of the day departed from Temple Meads at 5.10am. This job was one of the most detested duties at the depot, this was duty number 55 which was known as the 5.10 Avonmouth attached. Booking on time was 4.05am the usual 45 minutes being allowed for the preparation of the 55xx class. At 4.50am the Avonmouth engine went off shed attached to another 55xx class. The two locomotives then ran over to the old part of the station and hooked on to a five coach set which had been brought in earlier by the Dr. Days pilot engine.

Upon arrival at Avonmouth the train would stop just short of the crossover road. The fireman would then cut off the leading engine which just had enough room to run around the train with the level crossing gates closed. She then hooked on to a five coach set which had been waiting in the bay platform of Avonmouth Dock station, this train became the first service of the day to Severn Beach.

Duty 55 then went as follows - return to Avonmouth, Avonmouth to Severn Beach, Severn Beach to Temple Meads, Temple Meads to Pilning Low Level, Pilning to Temple Meads, relief, walk to shed, book off. During all those journies the locomotive took water six times. Any non arrivals were covered by men in the Junior Spare Link. Many a young fireman has cursed the very existance of the duty after being rousted out of a warm cabin to be faced with the sweat and hard work involved. Regarding the second engine which was left on the train at Avonmouth. This proceeded to St. Andrews Road station where the engine cut off, ran around through the town goods and reattached. A great deal of the workers off the night shift at the nearby smelting works would board this train. Departing at 6.15am this was a through train to Portishead. This was known as a Coast to Coast or inner Circle working.

One interesting job over the route occurred when one of the general managers of the GWR decided to take his annual holidays abroad. The usual contenders for this duty were 20xx Pannier tanks Nos. 2070 and 2135 which were two of the regulars. For this special occasion they would be given a good polish up by the B.R.D. cleaning gang. The general manager would travel down from London in his own private saloon, which was attached to the rear of the 9.5am express. This train arriving at Temple Meads at 11.25am. The saloon would then be detached and worked forward to Avonmouth with all haste by the gleaming little 'Twenty'. Upon arrival at Avonmouth the GWR engine would cut off and one of the Port of Bristol authorities saddle tanks which was fitted with a vacuum brake would then take the saloon and its passengers into the dockland, once safely inside, the G.M. would detrain and board an Elders and Fyffes banana boat which was bound for the sunshine of the West Indies.

Large engines were no strangers to the line. St. Philips Marsh 'Halls,' 'Granges,' 28xxs and RODs were familiar sights, as were Barrow Road 4Fs and class Fives. One B.R.D. duty was to work the 6.45 Plymouth as far as Taunton. Upon arrival there the Bristol men would report to the shed foreman then take to a 'Castle' or 'Hall' class which they would prepare and return with a stopping passenger to Avonmouth. One route went via Clifton Down whilst the other line diverged from Avonmouth at Hallen Marsh Junction. From here it climbed up past Chittening platform which was reopened during the war years. The bank continued through Blaise, there were sidings here during the last war for the storage of petrol tankers. The line then passes through Henbury station, Charlton tunnel and continues to climb until the top of the bank is reached by the Brabazon Hanger at Filton aerodrome. Just beyond this North Filton platform was reached with carriage sidings. Shortly after this the line went three different ways, straight ahead to Stoke Gifford West, right to Filton Junction and at one time left to Patchway, this short spur was lifted many years ago.

The water column at Severn Beach station was of the pull chain type, the fireman putting in the bag and pulling the chain to turn on the water supply. Coal pick marks made on the platform by previous fireman gave guide lines as to where engines should be stopped for water, whether running chimney or bunker first. A similar type of column was also situated at Hallen Marsh. During the Second World War an anti aircraft gun was situated some 200 yards away from this watering point. If a fireman was unlucky enough to be standing on the top of an engine when this gun opened up it would be a case of hanging on to anything solid, for anything in the area was shaken violently by its recoil. A passenger service still operates over the Clifton Down route as far as Severn Beach. Today it holds the distinction of being the only existing branch line service in the Bristol area. The Filton Junction route is now goods only. The section from Severn Beach to Pilning Low Level closed in 1964. Doctor Days sidings supplied the coaching stock for the Avonmouth duties. Two seven coach sets were kept at Clifton Bridge for dockers trains, these sets returning each evening to this stabling point.

Locomotives used over the route on passenger duties included all types of Pannier tanks, 45xx, 55xx, 41xx, 82xxx 2-6-2 tanks, Standard Goods and

No 5718 having just arrived at platform 1, Temple Meads with a train off the Radstock Branch, 25th February 1957. Fireman H. Vallis just visible on the footplate.   *(Author)*

GWR diesel railcars. With the once constant flow of traffic the kettle in the porters room at Avonmouth Dock station was always on the boil.

Last but by no means least we come to the Radstock or North Somerset branch. The depot was responsible for the following duties. The first train of the day departed from Temple Meads at 6.50am. The engine on this job ran light from shed to Malago sidings and picked up a train of "B" set coaches. She was then all stations to Frome via Radstock. Upon arrival at Frome she then went on service as far as Bruton. There she uncoupled, ran round and worked her train to Westbury. From there she returned to Bristol with a stopper over the Cheddar Valley line, a good days work for anyone.

The second duty was the 5.20pm Bristol to Frome returning once again over the Cheddar Valley line as far as Yatton. The stock was then put in the bay platform and the engine went on shed. The one Sunday duty was to work the 4.50pm to Frome, returning home at 9.29pm. The engine and crew standing at Frome for 3½ hours. All other passenger duties over the branch were handled by Frome men and one set of Westbury men. The Christmas day duty over the line was worked by a Standard Goods class engine. The reason for this being that this type of engine had enough water for the out and back trip. Should a freeze up occur or any other type of malady, this train could complete her service without hardship to the travelling public. Once again the versatile 55xx class saw a great deal of work over the line. During BR days the 465xx Mogul class put in several appearances. They were a poor substitute and were described as being as weak as robin. Bath Road men called them the 'Mickey Mouse' class.

Before the advent of the family car the railway was often the most direct and efficient way of getting to work. Many a docker, factory hand, mill worker and the members of the medical fraternity have been very thankful of the branch line services once operated by the men and locomotives of Bristol Bath Road shed.

Chapter 5

RED ALERT

For those who survived those grim and frightening years, the Second World War will always be remembered, to the railwaymen of this country it will be remembered for the long hours of duty, for the cautious travels during the blackouts and the bombing raids, the many extra duties and the run down condition of the locomotives long overdue for a visit to the shops. All this and

Pannier tank 4647 "raises the echoes" as it storms the bank between Radstock and Midsomer Norton with a Frome to Bristol working. (R.E. Toop)

more will be remembered, the 'Bulldog' spirit, the grin and bear it attitude also, helping our railways through this difficult and despairing period.

Not only were new duties gained, some were lost in the eventual reshuffle, Bath Road shed being affected in the following manner. The mid-day Salop went to Newton Abbot on a double home basis. A Wolverhampton duty over the North Warwick line was lost and the "Down Waker" disappeared from the sheds duty roster. This job being returned for Sundays only for a short period. To compensate this loss the two top links were given the following night duties. The 8.45pm returning with the 'Mail', the 12.10am Northern to Hereford returning with the Manchester and London Parcels to Swindon, returning from there with the ex-Leicester Parcels train.

Another new duty was the 10.00pm Passenger Pilot. The locomotive and its set of men being paid for by the Traffic Department. This duty varied. Sometimes the engine would not be used, it was merely kept as a stand-by. Should it be used to replace a failed engine the men would prepare another to take its place. On other occasions it was used to convey railway dignitories to the capital city. A rake of five Pullman coaches being stabled at Doctor Days for this purpose.

Regarding the 6.21pm London, during this period the engine rostered to this duty started from Taunton and worked a stopping passenger through to Bristol. She then returned to Taunton with a similar duty and then returned to Bristol where, Bath Road men gave relief in readiness for the London duty. With all the opening and closing of the dampers involved during the three previous journies the fire was generally in an unhealthy condition. This, plus a

49

tender of inferior grade coal made this a rough trip ahead for the Bristol men.

The men in the Super Spares Link covered a great deal of the extra wartime duties, they were also responsible for the working of the "Up Waker" on a Sunday night, returning home with the 9.20 off Paddington. This duty was often a struggle, for both man and locomotive. A Newton Abbot 'King' class was generally rostered to this duty. It had previously worked from Newton Abbot to Plymouth and from there through to Bristol. Very often an extra sleeping car would be put on at Temple Meads making the train the maximum load for this type of engine. A banker would be asked for, but owing to the shortage of motive power this was usually denied. That well known wartime term of "doing ones best" being put into practice. As the journey progressed the fireman would often have to dig the coal out of the fire iron rack or from around the water lid on the back end of the tender in order to reach London, such jobs being a nightmare for footplate men.

The men in the Super Spares Link also worked the many ambulance trains, these running to Avonmouth, Salop and Weston-Super-Mare to name but a few. One army Major involved with the movement of these trains is remembered for his kindness. This man always making sure that the footplate men were issued with a good cooked meal and a mug of tea each. Troop trains were worked to such places as Salop and Weymouth and prisoner of war personnel were transported to Eastleigh, where the engine, which was generally a 43xx, went on the Southern Railway shed to have the clinker removed from her firebox before returning. It could well be said without fear of contradiction that the men in the Super Spares Link won the war at Bath Road shed.

During the war the Weymouth road was kept open all night and one duty over this route is well remembered by the fireman involved. Engineman G. Cross and Fireman R. Hacker worked one of the U.S.A. troop trains from North Somerset Junction to Dorchester with a 63xx class engine. A Pilot man was picked up at Westbury to assist the Bristol men with road knowledge. At Dorchester the troops detrained, the fireman going through the empty stock with an empty sandbag for the well supplied Americans had left a wealth of "treasure" behind. Sugar, chocolate and tobacco — commodities which at this time were most difficult to obtain in this country. From Dorchester the E.C.S. was worked forward to Weymouth where the engine went on the shed there for turning, water and four tubs full of coal from the stage.

It was then decided that the empty stock should be worked to Old Oak Common (London) the Pilotman being dropped off at Heywood Road en route. The hard pressed fireman recalls the struggle involved lifting that tired old 63xx over Savernake Summit. London was safely reached, the Bristol men having worked just over 230 miles that day.

The blackout restrictions brought many difficulties when preparing locomotives at night. Flare Lamps were banned, only the feeble light from a gauge Glass Lamp being allowed. This made the oiling of the inside motion a very gloomy affair.

The A.R.P. sheets over and around the engines cabs not only kept the glow from the firebox concealed but they also kept the heat in, causing a great deal of sweat for the toiling fireman. These sheets also became a hinderance when swinging a fire iron from the tender rack. Out on the road they were a curse. One B.R.D. fireman miscounted the bridges out of Paddington and as he swung the pricker from the tender it made contact with the final bridge, knocking him flat on his back and out for the count. Other A.R.P. precautions included the removal of cab side windows and flaps were removed from the firehole. The doors being closed after each round of firing.

The City of Bristol received widespread damage from the German bombers. The first air raid taking place on 25th June 1940. Because of its importance Temple Meads station became one of the main targets. It was hit on 2nd December and the next raid which took place on 6th December was to become a night of terror for both passenger and railwayman alike. The 7.10pm Salisbury which was standing in the station at the time, received a direct hit. Both incendiary and explosives falling on the train causing many casualties. The train engine which was a 2-6-0, Mogul was heavily damaged.

Many acts of bravery took place that night. Without thoughts for their own safety, station staff, G.P.O. workers and locomen from the High and Low Level Pilots ran to the stricken train. Incendiary bombs were handled, men tore at the twisted remains with their bare hands to free the injured and the dead. Men came running from Bath Road shed as the word spread. Young cleaner boys gained first hand experience in the horrors of war. The dead were laid out in the subway, from here they were removed by the emergency services. That night of death and destruction will long be remembered by those who were witness to it.

On 3rd January 1941 a heavy incendiary raid on the station caused the Booking Office to be burnt down. The school at Barton Hill was hit by German bombs, a few of these falling on the nearby Doctor Days Sidings causing damage to both coaching stock and track.

Bath Road shed escaped damage. Two bombs landed in the garden of Clift House the D.S. residence, sadly killing a fireman and burying a driver in the rubble, luckily he escaped serious injury. One locoman lost his complete family in a heavy raid, but still reported for duty on time. Such is dedication. No.4036 *Queen Elizabeth* was the victim of a machine gun attack at Dawlish Warren with B.R.D. men on her footplate. Several cannon shells passing through her smokebox. After being involved in a few other incidents she was branded as being an unlucky engine.

The cave in the rockface beneath the Railway Institute building was used as an air raid shelter by certain members of the staff. Known as "Humpies Cave" it goes for many miles beneath the city and contains an underground spring. A familiar sight after a Red Alert warning was Shed Foreman Waterfield heading for this cave complete with a Gauge Glass Lamp to light his way. The alert calls for air raids were as follows:-

Yellow. Enemy aircraft over the coast. Blue. Enemy aircraft within the city. Red. Enemy aircraft overhead.

The cleaning of engines during the war fell to a rather motley gang. Italian prisoners of war were used, it is also said that it was them that introduced the long handled shovels for shed work. Soldiers being rehabilitated after injury were used as cleaners and women cleaners were employed at Bath Road and St. Philips Marsh sheds. Fireman Ivor Phillips who, after recovering from illness, was put on light duties at the shed was given the task of showing the ladies the job in hand.

On the night shift Ivor taught the newcomers the skills involved. The ladies were let loose on a 'Castle' class engine and their instructor recalls that his cleaners were unable to stand on the handrail to clean the top of the engine and that they did not venture beneath the engine to clean the gears. Three names remembered are Lily Williams, Amy Cambridge and Maud Bird. There was also a blonde lady employed at the depot as a boilersmiths mate.

Enginemen were required to take part in fire watching duties, such duties appearing on the depots roster sheet. Malago Vale and St. Annes being two of the principle places. During this period Bristol was visited by engines from the other three railway companies. Two regular visitors to Bath Road were a pair of ex LNWR inside cylinder 4-6-0's. These were stationed at Westbury for use on the ambulance trains. The LNER B12 class visited the depot for coaling especially at night, these too were used on the ambulance trains and had come off their trains at North Somerset Junction. The grates of these Eastern engines were designed to burn hard coal so when their tenders were filled with Welsh coal which was known as "blind" coal by other railways it could cause a few hair raising incidents for their firemen.

During this period the men on the 6am turning duty would book on at 4am to relieve the paper train. Sometimes this train would be a late arrival so the relieving crew would take refuge in the army canteen on platform twelve. Here they could enjoy a drink of tea, served in a jam jar. Even cups were classed as luxuries during this time of austerity.

A Lewis gun was mounted on the roof of the Loco Signal Box, it seems that this was done as a morale booster more than anything else. Throughout the years the 'King' class locomotives have been quite rare visitors to St. Philips Marsh shed but a wartime royal visit to the West caused two of the class to visit the Marsh. Wartime conditions did not stop Bath Road grooming one of their 'Kings' for this exalted duty. It was worked around to S.P.M. where it stood in the small side yard. Upon arrival of the royal train the Old Oak 'King' was cut off and went on shed. The B.R.D. 'King' taking over for the journey westward.

The work force at the Bristol Aeroplane Company went through a terrible ordeal when during a daylight raid very heavy casualties were sustained, the German bombers came back at a later date for a second attempt but this time the R.A.F. was ready. As the dogfights filled the sky so did the groups of railwaymen fill the yard at Bath Road shed to watch both fighter and bomber in their game of death. One of the fighters from a Polish squadron shot down one of the bombers, which went down near Duchess Ponds.

This small victory was received by the ardent onlookers at Bath Road, a loud cheer and flurry of caps filled the air, quite a few hats were lost that day. After the long hard struggle peace returned to our shores.

Let us hope that the dark clouds of war never visit our green and pleasant land again.

Chapter 6

LINES TO DORSET

Bath Road men had one regular weekday through train duty to Weymouth. This was the 8.05am which was in link 3A. Although this was known as the Diesel Railcar Line a few steam turns existed within it, nine drivers and four firemen covering such duties. The motive power on the 8.05 varied; 63xx, 'Halls' 'Granges', 'Manors', 'Stars', and 'Counties' all in turn seeing service over this route. 'Castle' class engines being used on heavier trains.

It was a well liked job for several reasons. It was a day turn so the hours were favourable, it paid two hours mileage and the load was reasonably light, seven or eight coaches being the maximum. The train catered for the markets which were open on certain days at various towns by stopping at these accordingly. Eight stations being called at as part of the normal service.

The following is a description of one such trip which was related to me by a fireman who was in link 3A during the forties.

"We booked on duty at 7.40am and walked to the station to relieve the men who had brought the 63xx and the empty stock in from Malago Vale Sidings. All was in order so at the appointed time we got the road and ran to Bath which was our first stop. Departing from there at 8.27am we left the historic city with its elegant Georgian buildings behind us and made our way through the wide sweeping valley. Eleven over bridges later we arrived at Bathampton and started slowing for the junction.

Our flanges protested noisily as we negotiated the right hand curve at the permitted 25 mph. A blast on the whistle for the farm crossing and our engine was opened up as we threaded our way through the winding course of the Limpley Stoke Valley. To our left high above us in the greenness of the woods was the tower like building of Browns Folley. Running on the embankment with the tranquil canal to our right we passed the ivy congested walls of Farleigh Manor. Shortly after this we passed beneath the first of the impressive stone built aqueducts which carries the Kennet and Avon Canal over the railway and into Conkwell Woods.

The junction for the Camerton branch went by which was closely followed by Limpley Stoke station. There were up and down loops there and a goods yard with three double ended sidings. A familiar sight there was the 20 ton coal wagons of Messrs Stevens and Clark which were easily recognised by the large white letters "S" and "C" painted on their sides. When a banking engine was not available for those heavy trains they reduced the load there before proceeding.

When a number of wagons had been assembled Westbury sent an engine and brake van down to make the stragglers into a train. A great deal of those trains would find their way to Southampton Docks, where at the Royal Pier they were unloaded. Some of this coal was supplied to the Isle of Wight. During earlier times many of the steam driven liners which sailed out of Southampton were "bunkered" with this coal. Salisbury men found regular employment on those trains, on a double-home basis from Severn Tunnel Junction with a 56xx class engine.

We made our way through the cutting on the long curve to Freshford, with Winsley Sanatorium perched on the hillside to our left. We passed through the diminutive Avon Cliffe Halt which held about one and a half coaches. There was an old pumping house there and a picturesque weir. We headed on through the trees to Bradford on Avon, our smoke rising up into the branches, and we rattled our way through the tunnel and over Green Lane Crossing. After crossing the river I would pick up the shovel and get busy as we attacked the stiff climb up to Bradford Junction. At the top of the bank we passed the distant signal. The drivers of goods trains kept a sharp lookout for this signal because the next one was obscured by trees. If the distant was at caution they would have to start holding up the train with the brakes.

Bradford Junction had a large triangle. The lines went left to Holt Junction and right to Trowbridge which was our route. We passed beneath another aqueduct then our Mogul got her head down for the climb up past the large loop. This loop was capable of holding three, sixty-wagon trains, the indicator showed the number of trains in residence. The brakes were applied and we came to rest in Trowbridge station. This was an important railway centre. To our left was the extensive goods yard which served Bowyers pie and sausage factory. A pilot engine was kept busy there on shunting duties.

To our right was the old engine shed and turntable by then silent and deserted. During the First World War two members of the 'Bulldog' class were stationed here, Nos. 3337 *The Wolf* and 3443 *Chaffinch*. During the 1914—1918 period many ambulance trains carrying service casualties from the western front were worked to Trowbridge by LSWR engines. From there one of the 'Bulldogs' would take over. Both these engines were kept in spotless condition. It was thought that a clean engine would help to cheer up the wounded men and perhaps, help them forget their terrible ordeal in those blood stained trenches.

The importance of Trowbridge was also shown in the fact that two London passenger trains started there. These were the 7.15pm and the 7.15am. The early turn was worked by a set of Westbury men, Bath Road men being involved with the evening duty. We would work the 5.10pm from Bristol and Trowbridge, unhook the engine, turn on the triangle and re-attach. We would then work the train forward as far as Holt Junction. Where we changed footplates with Reading men. They worked the London 'Up' and we returned to Bristol with their train.

A one minute stop was allowed at Trowbridge, the carriage doors were slammed, a whistle blown and our Mogul barked her way under the bridge and out of the station. My mate notched her up for the stiff climb up around Yarnbrook Signal Box, the line descending towards the distant signal for Hawkeridge Junction. The lines diverged, left to Heywood and right for Westbury. Over the "tump" we would go and past Westbury North Signal Box, where the West of England main line joined us. We ground to a halt as the hand on the station clock reached two minutes to nine.

Westbury was a very busy place. The station had two 'Up' and two 'Down' platforms, there were yards on both sides of the line and the smokey engine shed away to our left had an allocation of seventy engines. We departed at 9.03am and made for Fairwood where water troughs were situated. These could be either the second or the third set of troughs out of London depending on the route taken. The Old Oak men took a dip there as they headed for the West with their 'Castles' and 'Kings'.

We passed Clink Road Signal Box and climbed up to Clink Junction and where the main line went straight ahead we diverged to the right and made for our next stop. The line dropped sharply past Frome North Signal Box where the holding sidings for the Radstock coal and stone wagons from Mells Road and Frome quarries were situated. We went by the junction for the Radstock branch and came to a halt in Brunels station at 9.12am. There were two small yards on either side of the line, a goods yard and beyond this the timber built single road engine shed was situated. Although Frome was a sub shed to Westbury it was completely self contained having its own boiler washer etc. Two minutes later we were on our way.

Leaving Frome the road was level to Blatch Bridge Junction where we rejoined the West of England main line. Passing Woodlands Signal Box we climbed up to the Witham distant signal and on through the station, with the friary away to our left and the East Somerset branch winding away to our right. I got down to my labours as our Mogul barked her way up to the Brewham Summit Box. A change in the beat would tell me that we had passed beneath the bridge, then revert back to the familiar note as we went through Strap Lane Halt. The local push and pulls stopped there as they meandered down to Taunton.

Over the summit we went and ran down the falling grade which culminated in a 70 mph restriction around the notorious Sheephouse Crossing. We were now looking for the Bruton 'Down' distant signal. Bruton was a typical small country station with the college on the 'Up' side.

Still on the falling gradient we passed beneath the "Slow and Dirty" railway (S & DJR). Their Cole Station was situated above and to our left. Our next stop came into sight and as we rounded the curve my mate applied the brake for Castle Cary. There were 'Up' and 'Down' loops there plus the goods yard. The local push and pulls connected there with both 'Up' and 'Down' trains. Nice little jobs those, running through the serenity of the country side.

At the roadbridge the lines went their separate ways, straight ahead for Taunton and left of Yeovil and Weymouth. The line climbed and fell to Sparkford with the large sawmills there prominent to our left. On we went to Marston Magna where a large American camp was situated during the war. We ran downhill to a stop in Yeovil Pen Mill station. The triangle ahead of us was formed by the Weymouth, Taunton and Yeovil Junction routes, the engine shed being situated in the fork of the former of these. A handful of tank engines and a few diesel railcars were allocated there. The steam duties there included the Yetminster banker and pilot, the Yeovil station pilot and a stopping passenger to Trowbridge at night. The engine used on this job was turned out in immaculate condition.

As we waited in the station I banged a few shovelfuls around her, we got the tip and then climbed up beneath "Sunny Sams" Waterloo to the West main line (Southern Railway). We levelled of through Thornford Halt and started to lift our train up the bank. We went through Yetminster, where the banker was stabled. I have often wondered why with all the water available there, that the column was at Evershot. Knowing the GWR there must have been a good reason for it! We raised the echoes as we climbed through Chetnole Halt, the bank rising rapidly. The big lever was set in the 35% cut off position and the exhaust rasped out the chimney as we entered the tunnel. A familiar sight around there was the deer that frequented the area, but I was too busy bending my back to enjoy the delights of the scenery.

Just beyond the station the line fell rapidly away to Maiden Newton passing Cattystock Halt on the way. We went past the distant signal and stopped between the platforms of Maiden Newton station. This was the junction for Bridport, the branch which passed beneath the last arch of the overbridge, was often the domain of the 14xx class loco. The fodder trains that ran from Avonmouth stopped at such stations as this as they rattled their way to Dorset, very often a wheezing old ROD could be seen at the head of these trains. With the station work completed we got the right away at 10.10am. We left on the straight run to Grimstone tunnel with speeds of up to 60mph being allowed along this stretch. The beauty of Dorset could now be enjoyed, the county with the names to match its colour; Sandford Orcas, Cerne Abbas and Piddletrenthide. Through the avenue of trees we passed two of those deserted halts. Did anyone actually use those stations?

Plenty of 'Sound Whistle' (SW) boards were around for the numerous farm crossings. Tucked way in the trees to our left were the grey castle like buildings of Wolfeston House. With the chalk ridges above us we ran through the tunnel and into the market town of Dorchester. This was Thomas Hardy country, the famed poet. A line from one of his works reads, "In dry March weather we climb the road". Although written in a different period about a different road to ours it often seemed so very appropriate. We waited for the tip from the guard, the home signal and the catch points facing us. At the

Modified Hall 6991 Acton Burnell Hall climbs Bincombe Bank out of Weymouth with assistance from the rear, 11th September 1949. (D.K. Jones)

57

Mogul 7303 at Weymouth as viewed from Alexander footbridge, 15th June 1962.

(D.K. Jones)

appointed time we departed on the last leg of our journey.

We passed Dorchester Junction where the Southern Railway's line from Bournemouth and Wareham joined us by way of a sweeping curve, so we were now running over joint lines. We passed beneath the roadbridge and on to the high embankment, passing the cemetery and the cricket ground, with the main road running away to our right. We wound our way through the Dorchester hills, passing Monkton and Came Halt. We climbed for the final time up through the cutting, passing Bincombe Signal Box. This was usually the final drop off point for the banker out of Weymouth. Through the tunnel we went, 814 yards of it and as we reached its exit the regulator was closed and the brakes started going on for the descent down the 3¾ miles of the 1 in 51 Bincombe bank.

We dropped through the cutting, passing Upwey and Wishing Well Halt. On a clear day the view below us would be quite breath-taking. The naval base at Portland with all types of fighting power at rest, the sweeping curve of Weymouth Bay with the sun high-lighting its clear waters as far as the high cliffs of Lulworth Cove and beyond. Still braking we went through Upwey Junction where the Abbotsbury branch left the main line. The duties over there were covered by Weymouth men with one of their 14xx class engines. Still falling we went through Radipole Halt, the bank levels out as we passed Weymouth engine shed and we ran beneath Alexander footbridge, still slowing.

The Portland branch and the tramway to the landing stage went by on my mates side, a final touch on the brakes and we came to a stand in Weymouth

58

station at 10.33am. We had rung through for relief from Maiden Newton, and if we were lucky we would have two hours to ourselves. On this occasion we were not, so upon arrival I jumped down between the tender and the leading coach. Upon my call of "Ease up" my mate compressed the buffers and I dropped the coupling off.

The station pilot had attached to the other end of our train and as soon as the road was clear the empty stock was dragged away. We followed it out. The "Bobby" turned us across and we made for the shed. We went through the loco yard; I dropped down and pulled the necessary points to give us access to the turntable, where we turned our engine. Upon completion of this we filled the tank. Whilst my mate put a drop of oil around her I ran the bar through the fire and pulled some coal forward in readiness for our return. We then enjoyed a welcome can of tea in the enginemen's cabin. Our departure time from Weymouth station was to be 12.35pm, arriving home at 3.23pm."

The Bath Road number two mileage link had one Sunday duty to Weymouth. This departed from Bristol at 10am arriving at Weymouth at 1.25pm. Returning at 3.10pm and arrived home at 6.15pm. Weymouth shed was a three-road straight type building with a single road lifting shop alongside. During the late forties the allocation there consisted of the following types:-two 'Saint' class, four 'Halls', one 28xx, eight 53xx, one 45xx, three 1366 0-6-0PT (inside cylinders) and three Collett 0-4-2Ts.

The three 1366 class outside cylinder engines were for use over the Weymouth Tramway. This is the name for the stretch of line which runs from the station and winds its way through the streets to the landing stage where the Channel Island steamers operate from. Nos. 1367,1368,1370 were at Weymouth, the other three members of the class were allocated to Swindon shed for pilot duties within the locomotive factory there. Their 3ft 8in driving wheels making them very suitable for use over restricted curves. The Weymouth stud were fitted with coach heating apparatus and warning bells and were known locally as "Trammies".

Over the years a somewhat motley collection of engines have worked the tramway. During earlier times No. 1391 *Fox* an 0-4-0 tank engine from the West Cornwall Railway and No. 1337 *Hook Norton* of Hook Norton Ironstone Partnership Ltd origin, took care of things. A delightful little engine from the Bristol and Exeter railway, No. 1376 put in a long stay until being transferred to Oswestry in the late twenties, another home for oddities. The twenties period also saw the appearance of No. 679. She was a standard Peckett 0-6-0 saddle tank with outside cylinders and inside bunker which spent her life on the Alexandra Docks Railway at Newport. She remained at Weymouth until 1928 when she too left for Oswestry. Her stay there was short, being withdrawn in 1929. During the thirties it was the turn of No.

1331 from the ex Whitland and Cardigan Railway, yet another engine that found her way to Oswestry.

Perhaps the two most well known engines arrived on the scene in 1926. These were the ex Burry Port and Gwendraeth Valleys Railway Nos. 2194 *Kidwelly* and 2195 *Cwm Mawr*. As usual, they were fitted with the customary warning bells and the shunters step on the front right hand side. They were both kept in beautiful condition and although they came from an absorbed railway they had a definite Great Western look about them. They also held the distinction of being the only ex BPGV engines to wander afar from their native parts. No. 2195 left Weymouth in March 1939 when she was despatched to Swindon for scrapping. With the outbreak of the Second World War she became a war reserve and was reinstated in December 1939. She stayed within the Bristol division usually at Swindon making one brief return to Weymouth in 1945.

Sister engine 2194 stayed until 1940. After a brief spell at Cathays she was sent to Taunton where she ended her days. She was withdrawn in February 1953 after fifty years service, a credit to her sturdy design. Working instructions for rolling stock over the Tramway were as follows:— (Details being taken from the GWR General Appendix 1936)

With the exception of "articulated stock", corridor trains and coaches not exceeding 60ft 6½ins over buffers with 7ft bogies, passenger vehicles worked over this section must not exceed 9ft 3¼ins wide over projections and 59ft 4ins in length or a distance "centre to centre" of bogies of more than 42 feet or with an overhang from the centre of the bogie to the buffer of more than 10ft. The vehicles are marked at the ends WXQ and care must be taken that only such vehicles are allowed to work the Weymouth Quay. Passenger train vehicles of the corridor class worked over the tramway must have all the gangways and hoods properly disconnected and the doors secured (after which the screw couplings are to be slackened out and taken off for the loose couplings to be put on) before the train leaves Weymouth Junction.

The station despatching a train formed with coaches or vans of this description or if worked from a foreign line, the last stopping station before reaching Yeovil, must wire the Weymouth Station Master to arrange suitable staff to perform the work of uncoupling. As a matter of interest a single first class fare from Weymouth to Paddington in 1947 was forty one shillings and eight pence, and the charge for cabins on the Channel Island ferries during this period, including first class boat deck single berth, twenty five shillings; promenade and main deck two berth cabins, six shillings and three pence per berth. A regular boat train service ran from Paddington, Manchester (London Road), Wolverhampton, Swansea, Bristol and Plymouth on Tuesdays, Thursdays and Saturdays.

The GWR also earned good revenue from the potatoes and vegetables etc

Ex BPGVR No. 2195, 0-6-0 Saddle tank formerly named Cwm Mawr, on pilot duties at Swindon Works, 9th June 1949. She was employed on the Weymouth Tramway for many years, where she is still remembered with great affection. (Seaton Phillips)

which were shipped in from the Channel Islands. This merchandise was generally moved in "Perpot" box vans (perishable/potatoes). These trains ran to many parts of the country, Weymouth men running right away to London with them on a double-home basis. Regular visitors on these and the boat train duties were the members of the 83xx class. These engines were 53xx 2-6-0's with increased weight to the front end. All heavy trains required the assistance of the Bincombe banker which was generally rostered to one of the 53xx allocated to Weymouth shed but sometimes a 77xx was used on the banking duty. During weekdays the banker was stabled on either the sand furnace or lifting shop road. On Saturdays the banker was often kept in the goods yard. During the summer season as many as three bankers were in use.

On nights one set of men was kept on orders to work the banker if required, during the summer two sets of men would book on duty to work certain trains then return to their own duty. Although Bincombe Signal Box was generally the dropping off point some trains were assisted to the foot of the Evershot bank. The banker coming off at Yeovil and running round through the cattle dock. There was a cross over road at Bincombe and a middle siding for the storage of returning bankers. The Southern Railway bankers attached to the front of their passenger trains, class H15 and U class being used on this duty. A GWR 'Hall' class was allowed 288 tons for a single load over the bank.

Regarding the Southern Railway engines that could be seen at Weymouth, my own memory recalls Bulleid 'Merchant Navy', 'West Country' and 'Battle of Britain' Pacifics, 'King Arthur' and 'Lord Nelson' class 4-6-0's and the ex

LSWR 'Greyhounds' (T9 class). During later years British Railways Standard class engines were regular visitors. During 1958 a change in bounderies brought Weymouth under Southern Region authorisation, the shed code being changed from 82F to 71G, and from 71G to 70G in September 1963.

1967 saw the demise of Southern Region's steam locomotive stock. That last weekend in July 1967 all the remaining engines had to be assembled at three depots from where they would be officially withdrawn and despatched to various breakers yards. These three assembly points being Nine Elms, Salisbury and Weymouth. The last steam hauled train left Weymouth for Waterloo on the sunny Sunday afternoon of July 9th with Pacific No. 35030 *Elder Dempster Lines* in charge. As she climbed towards Upwey her whistle call faded into the distance and with it went part of our railway's history. Weymouth shed closed in July 1967, the last but one of the ex GWR steam sheds to do so.

The heart has been ripped out of Weymouth station and the pounding beat of the Bincombe banker is another treasured memory of yesteryear.

Chapter 7

CAPITAL CITY DUTIES

The Bristol—London route goes right back to the grass roots of the GWR. This was the first main line opened by the company, and this is why both these city's coats of arms are incorporated into the GWR's crest. Both these railway centres were to become key points on the network. Bristol with its two engine sheds with a combined allocation of just over two hundred locomotives handled a wide variety of passenger and goods traffic, whilst Paddington was to become the headquarters of the company.

The largest engine shed on the system was opened at Old Oak Common in March 1906. It was a massive four turntable roundhouse with some 230 locomotives being allocated there. It replaced the former depot at Westbourne Park which was of 1855 vintage. Trains from all over the network started or terminated at the capital. Paddington station had fifteen platforms which catered for both passenger and parcel traffic, the two longest platforms being 1,510 and 1,120 feet respectively. The station covers 15 acres in area and during 1947 it handled 340 trains daily.

All the GWR station clocks were checked against London time. The guards on the first trains out of London carried this time on their pocket watches and this in turn was related to each station master en route. The passenger services over this important route from Bristol were rostered to the men in the 'mileage link' at Bath Road. This is how the duties stood in the forties period.

9.0am Bristol, Bath, Paddington. 11.20am arrival, returning 1.15pm calling at Bath. Bristol arrival 3.37pm.

9.35am Paddington. B.R.D. men working this duty to Swindon, returning to Weston Super Mare with the 1.0pm stopper. Return working to Bristol. Relief.

11.45am Bristol and Paddington only via the Badminton route, returning home with the 4.12pm ex Paddington.

5.25pm Paddington. Returning with the same engine on the 10.10pm postal.

6.21pm Paddington, returning with the 11.50pm Penzance Sleeper.

Newton Abbot men had a return duty that departed from Paddington at 4.15pm. They were going home off a double-home duty with a fresh engine, generally a 'King'. During the war period many of the Bristol engines had reached a run down condition owing to pressure of work and as this train and the 4.12pm to Bristol were standing at adjacent platforms the Newton men would remind the Bristol crew that they would be breathing right down their tail lamp!

The Sunday duties from Bristol were 5.30pm Paddington returning with the 11.50pm and the 9.0am Paddington as far as Swindon, returning with the 1.0pm stopper. Other men working through Bristol with London trains were; Exeter men with the up Postal, Newton Abbot men with the up "Waker" and Laira men with the 7.45pm which during this period was the last train of the day. During earlier times Taunton men had a through working to London. Old Oak men also had return jobs.

To mark the centenary of the GWR the management decided to introduce a new express to link the two cities in a shorter time than ever known before. Hopes had been raised of a 90 minute schedule, but a booked time of 105 minutes in both directions was the eventual outcome. This new train was named the "Bristolian". The 'Down' train took the Bath route, the distance being 118.3 miles with departure time from Paddington being 8.45am. The Old Oak men that worked her down returned home with the 12.15pm Paddington. The 'Up' train which took the Badminton route, departed from Bristol at 4.30pm. This was the harder of the two routes with 2¼ miles of 1 in 75 of the Stapleton Road Bank and the long drag of 1 in 300 up to Badminton. Over this route the distance to London is 117.6 miles.

During the early days the train consisted of seven coaches comprised of the following stock; two third class brakes, three composites, one third and in the centre of the train one of the new buffet coaches. These coaches were of the latest wide type with recessed end doors. The weight of the pre-war train being 221 tons empty and 235 tons with the normal passenger load on board.

Castle class 4-6-0, 5025 Chirk Castle at Paddington Station with the 9.0am ex Bristol, carrying reporting number 455. (N.E. Preedy)

During the first months the duty was worked by the 'King' class with the streamlined 6014 *King Henry VII* putting in several appearances. It was soon found that the 'Castles' were capable of keeping time so the job became rostered to them. The duty was in the same link at Old Oak as the celebrated "Cheltenham Flyer".

The "Bristolian" was withdrawn at the outbreak of the Second World War but it was reinstated after the hostilities had ceased. Up to the winter of 1952-1953 no faster timing than 130 minutes was allowed. Once again the 'Kings' returned to the "Bristolian" duty, for by now the new BR stock had pushed the weight of the train up to 247 tons for seven coaches. By 1954 the 105 minute timing had been restored and the first 'Up' train was hauled by "His Majesty" himself, No. 6000 *King George V* with Engineman Walt. Flowers and Fireman D. Gardner in charge. Once again an extra coach was added to the train on Fridays.

When the 'Castles' became fitted with double chimneys and four row superheaters, both they and their single chimney sisters returned to the job. Regular engines were - 5048 *Earl of Devon*, 7014 *Caerhays Castle*, 7015 *Carn Brea Castle*, and 7034 *Ince Castle*, whilst 5076 *Gladiator* put in a brief appearance, but was somewhat erratic, 5062 *Earl of Shaftesbury* from Swindon shed put in at least one appearance.

The men in the link that worked the up train included — drivers Jimmy Russe, Ralph Stone, W.E. Brean, C.C.W. Iles, Bill Brown, H. Fowler, J. Harwood, Sid Wilkins, C. Nelms, A. Cook, B. Moore, S. Green and W. Huggins. The ranks of firemen included such men, K. Hall, J. Paine, V. Wilkins, B. Sture, R. Gazzard and D. Evans.

Being a prestige job the Bath Road cleaning gang kept the engine in gleaming condition, she was of course also kept in good mechanical order. Every night when the engine arrived on shed her fire was completely dropped, and after the necessary cooling her tubeplate, brickarch and firebox would be inspected by the boiler-smith. The first 'Castle' to be fitted with a double chimney was No. 7018 *Drysllwyn Castle* in December 1955. She is still remembered with great affection by the men at Bath Road. She was the fireman's engine as one man put it. Her exploits will go down in history for she holds the Blue Riband for steam when in April 1958 she whisked the up "Bristolian" to London in 93 minutes 50 seconds with the illustrious Jimmy Russe in charge. That will now stand for all time, a fitting memorial to a great engine. If there is a heaven for steam locomotives 7018 has certainly found a place there.

There was great rivalry amongst the "Bristolian" drivers, some would nearly hit the rivets out of the chimney in order to beat the best previous timing. This resulted in a good number of early arrivals at Paddington. A 'named train' punctually list was kept in the enginemen's lobby at Old Oak

Common. At the top of the list was the "Bristolian", but when the duty was handed over to a 'Warship' class diesel the honour fell to the number two on the list. This was the steam hauled "Inter City" (Birmingham-Paddington) with some brilliant locomotive work being put in by Tyseley men.

On 1st May 1958 Inspector J.F. Hancock rode on the 'Up' train and duly recorded an informative run. On the regulator was Engineman A. Giles and on the shovel was Fireman D. Gardner, the fireman kindly related that run to me, so let us return to that day and recapture the atmosphere of a typical "Bristolian" run.

Booking-on time was 2.30pm the roster sheet reading prep. 7018 4.30pm Bristol—Paddington.

Bath Road's favourite Castle, 7018 Dryslhwyn Castle receiving attention to her front end at Swindon Works, 3rd June 1956. She still carries an 87E (Landore) shed code plate, prior to her reallocation to Bath Road. The SC beneath this denotes Self Cleaning smokebox.

(N.E. Preedy)

The usual 60 minutes being allowed for the preparation of the engine, which on that day was a smartly groomed 7018. Her tubes had been cleaned on 30/4/58 and her boiler washed out 26/4/58. After the smokebox had been checked the cleaners would secure the reporting numbers and the headboard on the smokebox door.

The fireman that day continues with the story.

"Making sure that the sandboxes were full I turned my attention to the fire. The 'Castles' had a grate with the front bars sloping and the hind bars level, so a "middle" type fire was gradually built up in the box. Before leaving we had two 'drams' of coal put on the tender from the coal stage.

We went off shed at 3.30pm. Our guard was allowed walking time to the carriage sidings but he generally rode in the cab with us, so the order of the day was clean handrails and no pieces of clinker on the tender steps which could scratch his polished shoes. We ran tender first to Malago Sidings, where upon our arrival the shunter coupled us up to our rake of chocolate and cream coaches. The guard left us to join the train and I dropped down, lifted off the tail lamp and displayed "A" class headlamps on the front end.

At 4.0pm we were signalled out of the sidings and we ran gently to Temple Meads. We cautiously ran into platform nine and stopped behind the 4.15pm London which was still in residence there. I dropped the damper to keep her quiet and turned the blower just off the face to take the smoke away. Our guard came forward and gave us the load "247 for seven", he took down the necessary information from us and turned back down the platform. The final minutes ticked away, carriage doors were slammed, farewells were said, and the gold braid appeared on the platform to ensure all was in order.

On the stroke of 4.30 we got the right away, my mate replying with one on the whistle. We headed out through Dr. Days Sidings and just before Lawrence Hill I swung down the pricker bar and gave her a pull round. We passed beneath the Midland main line to Fishponds a few holes appearing down the front end, so I picked up the shovel and commenced firing. There was a good stock of 'Oakdale' in the tender and we had a good engine in our hands, so everything was in our favour. We went through Stapleton Road's lengthy platforms, the deep pounding beat from our 'Castle's' chimney reverberating back off the tightly packed streets of houses. We rattled across the bridge with the regulator two thirds open and cut off set at 27%. We attacked the 1 in 75 bank.

As we went past the large gasworks the crew of the little saddletank stop to watch our passing. We took the bank in fine style, leaving the city behind us. We were allowed 8½ minutes to clear Filton Junction. Albert checked his pocket watch as we went through the station. Our 'Castle' leaned to the curve, obeying the 40mph restriction imposed there. We ran on the embankment to Stoke Gifford. The west signal box was left behind, Albert opened her up as we passed the loops and the shunting yard where the St. Philips Marsh based Panniers were, as ever, busily banging about their duties. We headed out through the cutting as we ran to Coalpit Heath. Over the large viaduct we went to Winterbourne, passing over the LMS line, we sped through Wapley Common reception sidings and yard. Through the solid rock cutting we went at 70mph.

With the various overbridges flashing by we reached and passed the typical GWR country station of Chipping Sodbury. We gave her a dip as we passed over the troughs, having consumed 600 gallons since leaving home, we would also take a dip from the troughs at Goring and Streatley.

With a long warning blast on our whistle we plunged into the gloom of Chipping Sodbury Tunnel, this is 2 miles 913 yards in length and is ventilated by five air shafts that damp, musty aroma filled the air, but only for a few minutes for we were soon in the sunlight once again. We raised the echoes as we barked through the cutting, our rising smoke drifting down along the handrails as we went beneath the roadbridge and hammered through Badminton station at 70 mph—dead on time.

This station also served the nearby village of Acton Turville and was unique in the fact that the Duke of Beaufort, the local gentry had the powers to stop any through train at his own request. A stone built bank here was opened for the horse trials only. Badminton was also the final dropping off point for the Severn Tunnel bankers. They assisted this far with extra ordinary heavy loads or give that helping push to really rough running engines. Many a fireman on a weary old 28xx has been glad of the sterling work done by the 'Tunnel men' with their large Prairie Tanks.

That long drag of 1 in 300 ended here. The mileage post told us that we have 100 miles to go to our destination. We rattled through the short tunnel at Alderton and out on to the "racing stretch" as we called it. We went through another cutting, passing the Hullavington 'Up' loop. *Drysllwyn* was enjoying herself, the countryside had become a blurr of greens and browns, telegraph poles and hedgerows flashed by. Her coupling rods glinted in the sun, the roar from her double chimney was music to our ears. The clear ring from the ATC as signal after signal beckoned us on, we screamed through the station with the speed recorder showing 90mph. The cut off was the 20% position, the regulator two thirds open and my labours showed 210 lbs on the clock.

The large RAF station with its hangers buried in the grassy mounds flashed by, we crossed over the main road to Malmesbury and on past the greenness of Bincombe Woods. Albert was looking ahead for the Little Somerford distant signal, our Inspector was involved with his notes and clock watching while I was busy bending my back. The white hot fire danced on the bars as demanding as ever, with this type of fire, I threw the coal down the middle, keeping it loose along the sides.

Little Somerford was the junction for Malmesbury branch and at one time a branch to Dauntsey diverged from there. Traces of this could be seen passing beneath the viaduct. We raised the dust as we roared through the station at an ear shattering 96mph. The road levelled out to Brinkworth and we left the little red brick station behind in our slip stream at 90mph. It was not unusual for our 'Castles' to come through there at over the magic "ton" (100mph). Sometimes on this job they had to, to keep on time.

This was also the route taken by the South Wales to London "named" trains. The "South Wales Pullman", the "Red Dragon" and the "Capitals United Express" with gleaming 'Castles' from Landore and Canton were familiar sights over this stretch. The sound of the 'Britannia' class locomotives chime whistles drifting across the open countryside was also a familiar everyday occurrence. We climbed up around the curves to Wootton Bassett Junction, *Drysllwyn Castle* was slowed to 62mph. The reverser was wound back to the 45% mark and as we took the curve her flanges complained noisily. Perhaps in her way she was telling us that she wanted to run. Like an olympic athlete that takes to the running track with one objective in mind, our 'Castle' was full of eagerness for her duty in life.

We joined the main line and Albert opened her up, with an adjustment in the cut off she bounded away. Rushey Platt came into view, the old MSWJ crossed the main line there and, because of the bridge our distant signal had a sighting board behind it. We sped past the works, and the scrap yard, where engines whose working lives had expired awaited the cutting torch in silent lines. It was at these works that our 'Castle' and her sisters were built by Swindon craftsmen. Men in overalls stopped to watch our passing, some of these giving us a friendly wave.

Men in overalls threaded their way along the works road astride their bicycles, men in overalls were everywhere. The Swindon Works day-shift was going home. We were now 37½ minutes out of Bristol.

We were signalled 'Up' through the line, we went through the station at 78mph, the clock on the platform reading 7½ minutes past five, we were 1½ minutes up on the running time. By the time we reached Shrivenham, Albert had whipped her up to 84mph. Uffington was passed at 86mph with 215lbs on the clock, we crossed the division border line at Steventon in fine style at 83mph.

Didcot was reached at 5.25pm and with three minutes in hand we thundered past the towering power station at 82mph. At Goring I had the boiler full and as we went over the troughs my mate lowered the scoop and we replenished out tender with a mere 43½ miles to go. Over this stretch of line it was possible to make up lost time, still firing steadily we reached the "biscuit town" of Reading at 5.38½pm with 220lbs on the clock. Maidenhead put a stop to our gallop. Albert started putting the brake into her and brought her down to a crawl for a crippling 15mph speed resriction imposed 24miles 6 chains to 24miles 6¼ chains. As soon as we were clear of this restriction Albert opened her up to wipe out lost time which was now logged against us.

We roared through Slough at 72mph, passing the factories and trading estates. That cruel blow at "Maiden" had put us three minutes behind on the running time. By the time we reached Southall our 'Castle', in the skilled hands of Albert had cut the lost time to half a minute. Things on my side would now be taken a little easier. There was a good body of fire in her bowels so a few shovels full of small coal under the door would suffice. I could not run the fire down too low because *Dryslhwyn* had a return working from London. With a warning blast on the whistle we raced past Southall engine shed with a few 28xxs and 61xxs resting in the yard.

There was no let up for us as we went through Ealing Broadway at 70mph with the cut-off in 22% position and to show her approval *Dryslhwyn* blew off. At Old Oak Common we were still batting along at 70mph. Albert brought her back to 45% cut-off, suburbia was all around us and we slowed to 32mph through Westbourne Park. I kicked the damper down and assisted my mate with the signals. The Old Oak men were as busy as ever with their 15xxs and 94xxs on the moving of empty stock. They called theses duties the "ups and downs". We observed the 10mph restriction imposed on the approach to Paddington station, before coming to a halt at the Capital terminus.

I had allowed the boiler to drop to ⅛ full and the clock was back to 200lbs. I turned on the water feed, then the steam and adjusted the injector and filled her right up to the whistles. Up came our relief, the passengers left the train and walked past, some giving our engine an admiring look, whilst others went by as if she was not there. Although that speed restriction put us behind we had arrived a half minute early. We left our 'Castle' to the relief crew and we returned home with the 7.15pm. *Dryslhwyn* would return with the 8.15".

Although the pick of the Bath Road engines were used on the duty, a few failures occurred. One 'Castle' came to a dead stop at Wootton Bassett. A 69xx was sent down from Swindon to deputise. The 'Hall' put up a gallant fight, the roar from the chimney and the shower of cinders raining down on the carriage roofs must have been something to see. Sadly so much time had been lost that Bristol men missed their return working from Paddington. That 'Hall' arrived with more than one hot box. Another 'Hall' which stood in for a failed 'Castle' put in an excellent performance. This was 7904 *Fountains Hall*. She was in the loop at Hullavington and with an 'Up' South Wales goods. A quick change over was made and the train was soon underway. With Driver H. Fowler on the regulator this two cylinder locomotive wiped out the lost time and actually arrived at Paddington on time. Her only sign of this fast run was a hot leading crank bush.

Two minor faults with 7018 were as follows. In her early days in Bath Road there was no plate on the rear of the compartment that held the fire irons, so any overfilling of the tank resulted in a stream of water which was generally directed on the unfortunate fireman. It was also found that when she was working with the regulator ¾ open and the cut off at 25% the exhaust injector would not maintain the boiler level.

I will close this chapter by mentioning the demise of this once star performer. With the closing of Bath Road in 1960 No 7018 and her remaining sisters slipped away to St. Philips Marsh and by October 1961 she had been reallocated to Old Oak Common where she stayed until her withdrawal in September 1963. By this time she had become really rough riding and sadly neglected. She was put into store at Old Oak for a period of six months. She was then moved to Oxford for a further month. It was as if the authorities were loath to part with her, but like her sisters she was to become yet another victim of modernisation. She was dispatched to Cashmores of Great Bridge who put the final torch to her in June 1964. When she left this world she was a mere sixteen years old.

Chapter 8

SHED OPERATIONS

Although this book deals mainly with the Bath Road shed that I knew, the original Bristol and Exeter Railway depot also deserves a mention. This shed had both roundhouse and straight road stabling points, a large workshop and the company's offices also occupied the site. It was common practise for tender engines to be stabled on the straight road shed whilst the tankies could be found on the gas-lit roundhouse. Right up to its closure these two sheds were known as the "old broad and narrow gauge".

Saint class 2973 Robins Bolitho stands beneath the clock at the old Bristol and Exeter Railway shed, Bath Road. *(N.E. Preedy collection)*

A long walkway connected the shed with the road. At the end of this path was a large elegant clock which overlooked the yard. Below this a flight of steps descended to the yard. At the front of the shed the foreman's, inspectors and time offices were situated. To the extreme right of the running shed the workshops could be found, a hand operated traversing table serving these. A covered bridge connected the depot with the nearby divisional superintendants residence at Clift House.

Early GWR visitors to the B&E shed included 'Flowers', 'Atbaras', 'Dukes', 'Cities', 'Bulldogs', 'Saints', 'Stars', and 'Barnums'. Some elderly drivers still remember the 'Cities' with great affection. The three French compounds *La France*, *Alliance* and *President* are also remembered for their visits. Some of the shed foremen at the depot during the early twenties included Messrs. Wilkins, Phillips and Preston, the latter of these rejoicing in the nickname of 'Pepper'. This was because of his red hot attitude towards his job. One of the locomotive inspectors was known as 'Dripping'. The constant dew drop hanging from the end of his nose explaining this.

During the coal bonus days drivers often visited the depot on their rest day to check that all was in order. In those days drivers had their own regular engines and great pride was taken in their appearance. Dust sheets were placed over the boilers and even buffers and handrails were polished as a matter of routine. Such pride in the job stayed with some men even after life itself had ended. A grave in a local cemetery bears witness to this. A beautifully carved 29xx class adorns an old driver's headstone showing how strong a link can be formed between man and the steam locomotive.

During the late twenties a great deal of expansion and modernisation was planned for the GWR network. This scheme was sponsored by the government in order to reduce the mass unemployment which existed at this time. Temple Meads station which had become a most congested place, especially during the summer months, was greatly remodelled. Platforms were lengthened and additional ones were built. Electric signalling was installed in the central area and extra sidings and running lines were introduced. All this work blending in with the original Brunel station in a most satisfactory way. Bath Road shed was also to be rebuilt and its layout greatly improved.

The demolition of the old B&E was to prove a gargantuan task, our forefathers had built it to last. The large archway in the vicinity of the workshops did not give up without a fight. The first idea to bring the arch down was a good one but it was to prove a total failure as you will see. A member of the 28xx class, well known for their pulling strength, was chosen for this task. A sturdy chain was attached to the pillars of the archways and anchored to the twenty-eight's coupling hook. The engine was put into forward gear, the strain was taken and the regulator was opened. An almighty metallic bang shattered the hushed silence as the chain snapped. The archway look on unmoved at man's "feeble" efforts. More favoured demolition tactics were eventually used and success was gained.

The new engine shed was built on the site of the former workshops and upon its completion the old shed was abandoned and this too was demolished. The new shed opened for business in 1934 was a ten-road straight shed with all the usual facilities; time office, messrooms, stores, boiler house etc. The coal stage was equipped with three tips which coaled locomotives from the shed side only. The water tank which formed the roof held 135,000 gallons. The ramp beyond the stage was built on concrete beams and brick pillars. Just beyond this and hemmed in between the rear of the shed and the Bristol avoiding lines was the first of the over girder type turntables. All water was pumped to the depot from the River Avon at Foxes Wood. Seven water columns tending to the locomotives requirements.

Beyond the coal stage in an area known as the 'coalfield' the new locomotive works was erected. The 170 ft x 50 ft building boasted an overhead crane and a wheel lathe. Eight sidings in the coalfield were used for the storage of coal wagons and locomotives during busier periods. A second turntable was situated between the workshops and the high river walls. This enabled visiting locomotives to be turned without disturbing movements to and from the shed. Also in the coalfield area the gas house could be found. This building was opened by a Mr. Phillips who maintained that the smallest gasworks in the world was a clay pipe. Gas was produced here for the Great Western dining cars and gastank wagons were worked up from Weymouth and refilled here.

Bulldog class 4-4-0 3452 Penguin waits her turn to be serviced on the disposal road at the former B. & E. shed Bath Road.   *(R. W. Hinton collection)*

Bulldog 3407 Madras and 2-8-0 4701 rest in Bath Road Yard, 18th July 1935. Note the double stop block in the foreground. A 27xx Pannier tank reposes outside the Gas House, in the background. (R.S. Carpenter)

A few reminders of the Bristol and Exeter era survived the upheaval. The windows in the main wall on the Bath Road side of the shed were spared and for many years an old landing stage in the river could still be seen. This was a reminder of the days when coal was brought to the depot in barges. The allocation to the new shed was generally around eighty locomotives. During 1947 it was comprised of the following classes: seven 'Counties', four 'Saints', six 'Halls' (one oil burning), ten 'Stars', fifteen 'Castles', three 'Manors', three 53xx, two Standard Goods 0-6-0, five 41xx 2-6-2, one 51xx 2-6-2T, six 45xx 2-6-2T, nineteen 55xx 2-6-2T, one 14xx 0-4-2T, three 58xx 0-4-2T and one 20xx 0-6-0PT. Total 86.

No. 1014 County of Glamorgan freshly coaled at Bath Road, 12th June 1949. (N.E. Preedy)

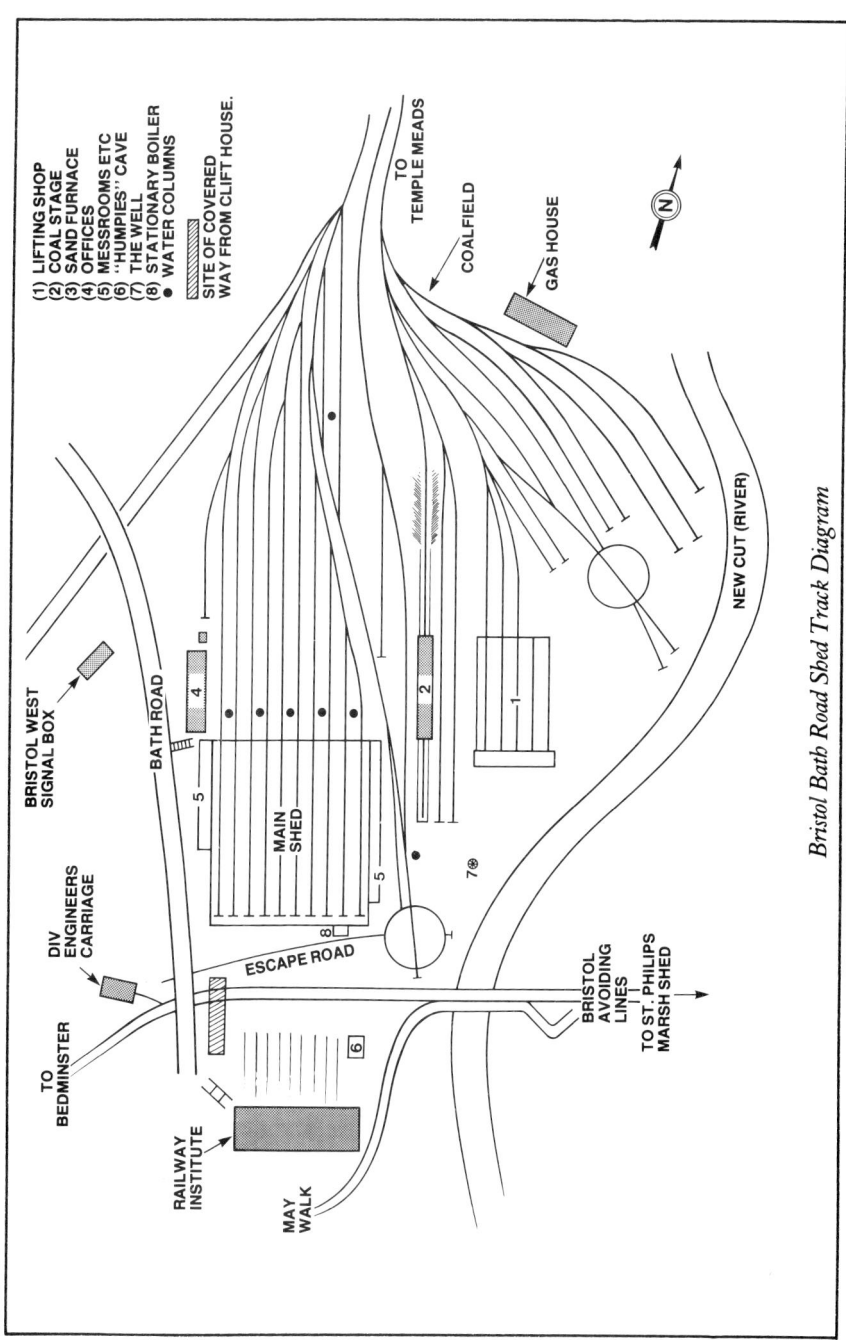

(1) LIFTING SHOP
(2) COAL STAGE
(3) SAND FURNACE
(4) OFFICES
(5) "HUMPIES" CAVE
(6) MESSROOMS ETC
(7) THE WELL
(8) STATIONARY BOILER
● WATER COLUMNS
▨ SITE OF COVERED WAY FROM CLIFT HOUSE.

TO TEMPLE MEADS

GAS HOUSE

COALFIELD

N

NEW CUT (RIVER)

BRISTOL WEST SIGNAL BOX

BATH ROAD

MAIN SHED

4

2

1

5

5

7 ●

8

ESCAPE ROAD

DIV ENGINEERS CARRIAGE

TO BEDMINSTER

RAILWAY INSTITUTE

MAY WALK

6

BRISTOL AVOIDING LINES

TO ST. PHILLIPS MARSH SHED

Bristol Bath Road Shed Track Diagram

A general description of these various engine class duties was as follows:

'Hall' class
General duties. Salop, London, West of England, Salisbury and Weymouth. During the Second World War period they did sterling work on ambulance train duties

'Grange' class
General duties, greatly favoured over the Weymouth and Salisbury roads, with their 5ft 8in coupled wheels they were very useful on this type of stopping passenger. I cannot ever remember any 68xxs being allocated to the depot but they were frequently on loan from St. Philips Marsh and were regular visitors from other sheds.

'County' and 'Castle' class
All general and mileage work over all routes.

29xx 'Saint' class
All duties including occasional relief work to London. During their final years they were hard work, when used on such trains as the 5.45am and the 8.10am Salisburys, both these being heavy trains with a great deal of stopping involved.

40xx 'Star' class
All duties. During their declining years they could often be found on stopping passenger and parcel trains.

78xx 'Manor' class
During the week the BRD 'Manors' were employed on such duties as the 5.25am Taunton milk train and on stoppers to Swindon, Cardiff, and Taunton. On weekends they were used regularly on the 12.10 Hereford over the Ross on Wye route.

45/55xx class 2-6-2T
Branch line, local and passenger duties (auto fitted - Yatton—Clevedon)

41/51/81xx 2-6-2T
Heavier trains over the Avonmouth road including the ex Clifton Bridge docker's trains.

14xx 0-4-2T
Yatton branch and coach shunting duties.

58xx 0-4-2T
Blagdon branch and coach shunting duties.

20xx 0-6-0PT
Coal yard and station pilot duties.

General view of Bath Road depot, 9th July 1960. The large building to the left, behind the coal stage incline is the lifting shop. (D.H. Ballantyne)

Double bar Pannier tank 2072 of 82A (Bath Road) passes her home shed on 26th May 1951. Built at Wolverhampton in 1899 she was called in for scrapping from Birkenhead shed in 1956. (R.W. Hinton)

Manor class 4-6-0, 7801 Anthony Manor of Chester shed, at Bristol Temple Meads, 29th August 1954 on a running-in duty from Swindon.

(R.W. Hinton)

Members of the 60xx 'King' class were regular visitors to the depot and over the years the following examples were allocated to BRD. Nov. 1939 to 1943. 6011 *King James I*, during 1949 6018 *King Henry VI* and 6019 *King Henry V* were at the depot. 6026 *King John* was there from Nov. 1939 to April 1943 and finally the celebrated 6000 *King George V* was at BRD during 1952. Their duties from Bristol varied. Some shed foremen put them on the 6.30pm stopper to Swindon, with other 'King' duties including the 5.25pm London, returning with the 'Down' postal. The engine used on this job generally worked the 6.25am to Newton Abbot the following morning. They were also frequent visitors on the Sunday morning "Down Waker" to Plymouth.

Individual locomotives are remembered for various reasons. Some were worshipped whilst others were hated. 4096 *Highclere Castle* was considered by some enginemen as being the best 'Castle' at the shed. Other good steamers included 5019 *Treago Castle*, 5025 *Chirk Castle* and 5048 *Earl of Devon*. During the BR double chimney regime No. 7018 *Drysllwyn Castle* was top of the list. She was considered by many firemen as being the mistress of her trade. On good Welsh coal it was claimed she would run to London with the firebox doors open! During the fifties many of the ageing 'Saints' and 'Stars' ended their days at the shed. A good deal of them had reached a run down condition. Several coats of grime covered their paintwork, they had become unkempt, rough riders and poor steamers. Their days of former glory were now a cherished memory of yesteryear.

One such "duffer" was 4047 *Princess Louise* her poor steaming had brought her to be known as 'Princess Lousy' by Bristol men. She could be generally found at the head of the four coaches that formed the 7.48am Taunton passenger. This train stopping at fifteen stations on route. Every morning would find her crew coaxing her from one station to the next, enginemen claiming that she had only one tube unblocked and that was to let the smoke out. Upon reaching Taunton 4047 would have a lengthy rest period before doing battle on the return working. It was during one such rest period that fate was to play her hand and thrust greatness upon the ageing 'Star'.

News had arrived of a 'King' class in trouble. She was returning home to London and was suffering from a bogie hot box. A replacement engine was needed to work the London forward so 4047 was chosen for this task. The Bristol men set about preparing her and with the blower screwed hard on they even managed to get her blowing off! Perhaps old *Princess Louise* was recalling happier times when she was a top link express engine. She was taken to the station and the change over with the 'King' was made. The Bristol fireman Ron Hacker wished his cockney counterpart luck, he was going to need it on that old camel. The old lady was soon underway, she would try her best to make up some of the lost time. The Bristol men watched her go out of the station and hopefully out of their lives forever, but this was not to be.

The following morning the two Bristol men booked on duty for the 7.48am Taunton as usual. Their hearts sank for there, quietly gurgling to herself outside the time office was *Princess Louise*. The sad story was soon related to them. She had got as far as Athelney and stuck for steam. Even the might of Old Oak Common had failed with her. A 42xx 2-8-0 tanky was commandered off a goods train at Westbury to work the ill-fated London forward. 4047 was finally called home for scrapping in July 1951 after 37 years service. In the ranks of enginemen her passing was not a sad occasion. Other members of the 40xx 'Star' class allocated to the depot in August 1950 were the following:- 4020 *Knight Commander*, 4033 *Queen Victoria*, 4034 *Queen Adelaide*, 4035 *Queen Charlotte*, 4041 *Prince of Wales*, 4042 *Prince Albert*, 4043 *Prince Henry*, 4056 *Princess Margaret*. As a young spotter I saw all the remaining 'Stars' except two, these being 4007 *Swallowfield Park* - originally *Rising Star* (85A) and 4023, a non named engine - originally *King George*, from Landore shed.

No. 4041 *Prince of Wales* will be remembered as being the engine that arrived at Temple Meads with a London train, where upon stopping, her smokebox door swung open. It was discovered that the dart on the securing handle had burnt right through. One of my own memories is of an unkempt No. 4056 *Princess Margaret* dwindling away her final days. When my class at school visited the Festival of Britain in London in 1951, 4056 was at the head of our train. This gave me a great thrill, the cleaners had given her a rub over and she looked a real picture standing under the overall roof of Paddington station. How I wished that I had owned a camera in those far off days.

It gave me great joy when I heard that 4003 *Lode Star* was to be put on show in Swindon museum for all to see, for during their hey day they were 'Stars' indeed. It was during a visit to Swindon Works in 1951 that I had seen 4003 last. She had been withdrawn from Landore shed and was not the cleanest engine on the works by any means but she was one of the proudest.

Over the years a good deal of the 'Hall' class saw service at the depot. Nos 6971 *Athelhampton Hall* and 6972 *Beningbrough Hall* were delivered brand new to the shed in 1947. 6971 was eventually transferred to Tyseley where she became a regular on the Swindon parcels duty in their No. 5 link. 6972 remained at Bath Road until its closure. She was then reallocated to St. Philips Marsh. She was withdrawn in March 1964 and put in store until May 1964. Her last journey was for cutting up by Hayes of Bridgend. She had witnessed the end of Bath Road and missed the closure of St. Philips Marsh by a mere fortnight.

Some engines were to see service at all three Bristol sheds. No 6997 *Bryn-Ivor Hall* and 6982 *Melmerby Hall* were both at BRD, SPM and then ended their lives beneath the shadow of the gasworks at Barrow Road. One of my favourite engines No. 4914 *Cranmore Hall* spent her life at both Bath Road and St. Philips Marsh between July 1949 and December 1963. This was the

No. 6902 Butlers Hall in the Bath Road coalfield with sister engine 6972 Beningbrough Hall, on a running-in turn from Swindon Works, June 1958. (L.C. Jacks)

date of her withdrawal, she lingered on in store at the Marsh until the following February when she was towed away for scrapping. Birds of Risca putting the final torch to her. When I was an engine cleaner at St. Philips Marsh I spent many pleasurable hours polishing her brass and copperwork.

Other new engine deliveries to the shed included 2-6-2 tank engines Nos. 4151, 4152 and 4155 in 1947 and No. 7019 *Fowey Castle* in May 1949, at this time No 7018 *Drysllwyn Castle* was delivered new to Landore shed. When the Temple Meads—Acton class C goods was restored to a double home working after the war No. 5025 *Chirk Castle* was taken around to St. Philips Marsh shed for the first peacetime run. During 1938 one of the old 'Duke' class No. 3291 *Thames* could be found on the BRD allocation list. Codes for the Bath Road depot were as follows— 22, BL, BRD and finally 82A. When the new depot was opened in 1934 the code became BRD but before this engines from both the Bristol sheds carried the BL code.

Regarding the shed duties this is how the "links" stood in the late forties.

Link Number	Duties
One and Two	Mileage links, 13 turns of duty in each. Paignton, London, Cardiff, Salop, Salisbury, Weymouth and over the Berks. and Hants. route with such trains as the 11.22am Reading. Three long and three short journies being a weeks work ie three Salops and three Salisburys.
Three	Cardiff and Salisbury twelve turns.
Three A	Diesel railcar link. Eight turns, one Weymouth duty with the twin cars Nos. 35 and 36 (sometimes a steam engine duty).

Link Number	Duties
Four	"Round the circle link". 13 turns including Cheddar Valley and Radstock
Five	"Clifton link", 12 turns. Portishead, Avonmouth, Severn Beach, and Pilning low level.
Super spares	12 turns. Covering all mileage work. For knowledge of the road men worked the 9.0am Paddington from Monday to Saturday. For West of England road knowledge men worked the 5.45pm Plymouth on Sunday. One fully fitted freight was once incorporated into this link. This was the 7.10pm Temple Meads and Tyseley, Bristol men booking off at Wolverhampton. In later years men booked off at Gloucester. Once a firemen had entered this link he never returned to St. Philips Marsh.
Junior spares	12 turns. Covering all jobs in the Clifton link and any short distance work which became available.
Workmans	12 turns. A great deal of this work was over the Avonmouth and Portishead routes.
Shed	Turning and stabling locomotives at Bath Road and St. Philips Marsh sheds.

Men in the Bath Road shed link were dispersed in the following manner. One driver and fireman bringing in locomotives from the coalfield and the coal road to the coal stage. From here another set of men took over and were employed on turning and taking the engines to the sand furnace. From this point another set of men stabled the engines either in the shed or on the roads one to ten or on the two outside roads Nos. 11 and 12. Roads 2 and 3 seemed to have been favourites for boiler washouts. The concrete in the bottom of the pits showing far more signs of wear caused by the pressure of water released from countless mudhole doors over the years.

When ever possible the GWR Bristol sheds worked to the following system. An engine was due for a boiler washout after ten days in service, a system using the last digit of the locomotive's number determined the date. For example No. 4096 would be washed out on the 6th 16th and 26th of the month. Unfortunately engines became overdue owing to pressure of work and use by other depots etc. From time to time Swindon would send out a list of overdue engines, these would be stopped wherever they were to receive attention. For the guidance of the staff, engines requiring washouts, firebox repairs etc would be marked in chalk by the shed runner on the cab side. Some of the abbreviations used were — *W.O.* wash out; *N.F.* no fire; *allout*, fire to be completely dropped; *die out*, allow fire to go dead; *boiler M/T* boiler empty;

The Bath Road Shed Link pose for their photograph in front of No 5094 Tretower Castle. Left to right: Con Smith (driver); Tom Senior (foreman); D. Jones (fireman); G. Goodland (fireman); W. Harris (driver); P. Jones (fireman) and Driver Tommy Shakespeare.

(Author's collection)

cripple, failed or engine for repair. Such legends as no brake being self explanitory.

At the commencement of the Second World War the coach shunting duties were returned to the shed from St. Philips Marsh. This was done in order to keep the strength of the shed up and also the foreman's rate of pay. These duties were as follows - West Sidings pilot (three turns) additional pilot on duty between 6pm and midnight. Doctor Days pilot (three turns). One regular duty was known as the 'Under the Wall' pilot. An additional pilot which shunted the signal box side of the siding went to shed at 1.0am. Stock brought in to Temple Meads by the Dr. Days pilot included the 5.10am Avonmouth and the 5.25am Taunton. Other duties in the "coach banger" link included the Malago Vale pilot, three turns of duty here, early midday and evening. S.P.M. men which often worked on these turns booked on at 6.32pm and walked to Malago and relieved the midday men. The last duty of the day for this engine was to stable the stock of the ex 8.44pm Crewe which arrived at Malago at around 1.30am. The pilot often returned to shed attached to the Crewe engine.

Last but by no means least there was the coal yard pilot. For many years this was the domain of No. 2031. She was a member of the delightful 2021 class being built at Wolverhampton Works in 1897. Bath Road had found this duty

The fish dock pilot worked at the East end of Temple Meads station. No 8795 rests between duties, 9th Marsh 1958, displaying the correct four-lamp code. *(Author)*

for her, away from the hustle and bustle of the main line. Perhaps the heirarchy had some respect for her age. For the early duty, men booked on at 7.30am and removed the empty wagons from the coal stage replacing these with full ones. The empties from the previous twenty four hours would be formed into a train and worked to St. Philips Marsh shed via North Somerset Junction, the yard shunter acting as the guard on this train. The pilot would then return with loaded wagons of coal which would be berthed in the Bath Road coalfield.

An old round windowed GWR brake van was used on these trains, the brass beading round its windows being kept in a very highly polished state. She was another old timer relegated to this quiet backwater. The afternoon men started their duties at 3.0pm. They would clear and reload the stage at 5.30pm. This final shunt would keep the stage going until the following morning. The sight and sound of old 2031 charging the coal stage incline was certainly a thing to remember. During March 1945 another veteran was allocated to the shed. This was No. 2709 of 1896 vintage and she ended her days on the coal yard pilot being called in for scrapping by Swindon in November 1948. For the record, 2031 ended her days on the Cannons Marsh pilot. Three men were employed on the coal stage and during the height of the summer season they would get through 140 tons of coal per shift. Some of the coal grades used by the GWR included Oakdale, Markham, Taff Merthyr, Bargoed and Six Bells. Three firedroppers and one ashpan and smokebox man took care of the other duties on the disposal road.

By 3.0am the shed would be packed solid with locomotives and every smoke chute emitting forth a black plume into the atmosphere from its occupier. As the early hours crept by the tranquility turned into feverish activity. As the city of Bristol prepared for another day so did the men of Bath Road as they got on with the job in hand getting the engines ready that would haul the trains and take many Bristolians to their places of work. Workmans, local passengers and early morning pilots all being prepared in the smokey shed. The sound of blowers, the gurgles of the injectors, the wild dancing shadows as the flickering flare lamps lit up the darkness on the winter's morning, engine after engine going off shed to start another days work. By 6.30am the shed would be virtually empty except for the washouts and the few engines for the later duties such as the 9.0am London.

During the late forties there were 130 sets of enginemen at the depot. At one time a floating link of twelve men was formed. This link comprised of Bristol men that had been sent away from home to be made up. The floating link only operated during the summer season. The following grades of office staff were employed per shift. Two booking-on clerks, two duty sheet clerks, these men also dealt with sickness, holidays and the spare men. There was also one Chief Clerk, one of these being Mr. Caslin. Other grades employed on shed operations included - one storeman and clerk, two steam raisers, two sets of boilerwashers on days and one set on nights, one cookhouse attendant, one A.T.C. electrician who was responsible for the charging of the locomotive batteries, one brakeblocker and mate.

The supervisory grades included, one chief foreman, one shed foreman and one foreman fitter. There were also three locomotive inspectors who had their own office. No matter how mundane some of these tasks must seem they were all essential to keep a railway running. So much has been recorded about the top link passenger drivers, so let us spare a thought for men like the shed labourers and drainmen. One of the shed's main drains was behind the lifting shop. To us young cleaner boys it was a fearsome place. When we were assisting the drainman we would cautiously peer over its edge, some saying it was twenty feet deep. We called it "The Well".

Several of the Western Region's named train services passed through or terminated at Bristol. The following headboards could all be seen during the steam era.

1. **"The Bristolian"**. 'Down' train worked by Old Oak men departing from Paddington at 8.45am, 'Up' train departing from Temple Meads at 4.30pm arriving at Paddington at 6.15pm. Train reporting numbers for 'Down' trains were 116, 119, and in the final days of steam 212. 'Up' trains carried 473. On the odd occasions 017 has been carried.

2. **"The Cornishman"**. Before 1939 Stafford Road man and engines worked the train double home to Plymouth. The engine in those days was generally a 29xx or a 'Star' class. Laira men providing the balancing service to Wolverhampton with their engine. After the war the S.R.D. engine worked through to Newton Abbot, the men having relief at Bristol. The Stafford

Road men relieved the Bath Road men on the return "Cornishman" working which they had worked up from Newton Abbot. A 'Castle' was the booked loco on the duty during this period.

In 1952 the duty was altered to an "out and home" working. The train was then 9.15am off Wolverhampton arriving at Bristol at 12.28pm. The engine came off at Bristol and the train was worked forward by a Newton Abbot engine and men. Arrival at Penzance was 5.55pm. The balance duty left Penzance at 10.30am on the same day. One engine in regular use on this duty was 5047 *Earl of Dartmouth*. She was the first Stafford Road 'Castle' to be fitted with water treatment by Houseman and Thompson.

Despite the long mileage involved (223 miles) the "Cornishman" was never considered to be a crack job. It was in link No. 4, the lowest passenger link at Stafford Road shed. During the last years of steam traction 7026 *Tenby Castle* was a regular on the duty. She is remembered as being a somewhat erratic performer. When members of the 10xx 'County' class were allocated to Stafford Road these in turn saw duty on the "Cornishman".

After 1952 the train was routed from Wolverhampton via the main line to Hatton North thence to Stratford via the Bearley branch. Before that it went via the North Warwick at Tyseley. Reporting numbers generally carried were 675 and 849. In later years C35 was often carried. During the fifties 70023 *Venus* was a regular engine on the Newton Abbot duty from Bristol. Typical of the Newton engines she was in immaculate condition and well maintained. During the summer service Newton Abbot was a fantastic place to be. It was a very sad day when this once busy shed lost its engines and men in 1981.

3. "The Merchant Venturer". Inaugurated in 1951 this train departed from Paddington at 11.15am terminating at Weston Super Mare. The return train departing at 4.35pm. Generally a 'Castle' on this job, but the two 'gas turbines' both put in appearance. The train reporting number was 142. On odd occasions 209 and 020 was noted on the smokebox door.

4. "The Devonian" This train was worked from Bradford to Bristol by a Midland Region engine, a West country 'Castle' taking over at Temple Meads and working the train forward to Paignton. Between May and September the train worked through to Kingswear.

For completeness I will mention two named trains that only ran on special occasions, the first of these appearing in the fifties. This was the "Bristol Holiday Express", which ran for limited periods only during the summer. Generally for periods of one week at a time. A different destination every day was an added attraction. This, plus the cheapness of the fares made it a very favourable way of spending a holiday.

Some passengers booked the same compartment for the whole week and to add to the holiday spirit they decorated it with brightly coloured streamers, although the train was cleaned at the end of the day these decorations were left intact by the cleaning staff. I think the engine carried a headboard, the carriages certainly carried the train's name on the destination boards on the sides of each roof. The second of these trains to carry a headboard for a short time was the regular service 9.5am Paddington to Bristol. This occurred between the 3rd and 13th June 1959 to commemorate the Bath Festival.

Bristol has been graced on more than one occasion by visits from our Royal Family. The following is an accurate account of one such visit by the Duke of Edinburgh on 5/6th November 1953, Bath Road engines and men being involved in part of this operation. The Royal Party travelled by special train from Edinburgh to Filton Junction station. The return train running from Temple Meads to Paddington departing at 4.15pm. Both these train running under "Deepdene' arrangements. The preparations for the two days were as follows.

Working of the special train early morning 6th November. Driver S.W. Grainger and Fireman S.V. Hawsbee booked on duty at 7.0pm at B.R.D. then travelled as passengers on the 7.15pm Shrewsbury arriving there at 10.25pm. The two men then walked to Coleham shed to prepare engine 5073 *Blenheim* (84G). She had been coaled with grade 1A Oakdale coal. This engine went off shed at 11.45pm chimney towards Hereford, proceeding to the turntable siding at Severn Bridge Junction arriving there at midnight. When the LMR engine had brought the special train to a stand in Shrewsbury station and gone to shed, 5073 was attached to the rear of the train departing from the station at 12.55am. She then worked the train to the stabling point at Westerleigh Curve West.

Later on that morning Driver C.C.W. Iles and Fireman S.S. Heales booked on at Bath Road and took to the readily prepared 5000 *Launceston Castle* (82A) going off shed at 3.50am tender leading to Stoke Gifford. Upon arrival at her destination 5000 then followed the special train to the stabling point, No. 5073 unhooked and was released to Bath Road shed via Yate South Junction No. 5000 then attached and remained on the train for steam heating purposes. Instructions to enginemen stating that engine noises in the vicinity should be kept as quiet as possible.

At 10.0am 5000 and train left the stabling point and worked to Filton Junction station. Here the Royal Party detrained. Engine 5000 then worked the empty stock to Dr. Days sidings and was released to Bath Road shed. The 4.15pm return train was worked forward by 6001 *King Edward VII* with Driver A. Ellsworth and Fireman A.H.P. Mitchell in charge. One of the Bristol men involved recalled that on the platform's edge at Filton Junction station someone had painted a white line, when the train engine stopped the engine's gangway had to correspond with the said line. By doing this the red carpet would be in line with the carriage door of the exalted party. As usual with such special duties all the engines involved were turned out in pristine condition.

From notes I recorded when I was a cleaner at S.P.M. the following 2-6-2 tanks were reallocations to Bath Road, some of them were still carrying their former shed codes. In December 1957 No. 4553 of Pontypool Road was on shed. Other engines on the eve of their reallocation were 5188 from Stafford Road July 1957, auto fitted No. 5529 from Barry February 1958, 5527 from Cathays July 1958. Other notes include 6107 as ex works in BR green livery 8/2/58 and 82007 on shed 15/1/59 carrying no shed plate.

During October 1957 No 4577 became derailed and plunged down the bank at Malago Vale sidings. She ended up in rather battered condition and covered in mud. She was outside the loco factory on the 30th. Her right hand side and front buffer were the worse for wear. Several days later she was moved down to the dead end road behind the coal stage. Just after this I lost track of her whereabouts and the next time I saw 4577 she was back in service complete with a repainted smokebox. This was on 3rd December 1957.

During March 1958 the Bath Road coal stage became blocked, (the reason why escapes me). This resulted in many of the in coming engines being sent to St. Philips Marsh for coaling. During the summer months many of the S.P.M. 4-6-0 locomotives were loaned to Bath Road for excursion working. As I said earlier the 68xx were very popular, 6811 *Cranbourne Grange* and 6852 *Headbourne Grange* becoming two favourites. With the introduction of British Railways green livery many of the smaller classes became thus treated. One example was No. 6327 which was turned out from Caerphilly Works on 28/5/57 complete with polished safety valve cover and a red painted reverser

Mogul 6372 on a running-in duty from Swindon in May 1956. Her appearance in BR green livery caused quite a sensation amongst the enthusiasts at Bristol that evening! (Author)

bar, a real picture she looked. The spies must have been out for by October she had been whisked away to B.R.D. for passenger work. She was returned in May 1958 by which time inches of grime covered her paintwork and steam leaked from every joint. By the look of her she had earned every penny of her revenue.

The first two 63xxs to be painted in BR green were 6372 and 6385. The former of these arrived at Temple Meads one evening in May 1956 on a running-in duty from Swindon. She was quickly surrounded by admiring enthusiasts. Although she had a BR emblem on her tender her green livery stirred up memories of glorious Great Western Days.

Chapter 9

MEMORIES FAR AND WIDE

I feel that this book would not be complete without mentioning some of the stories relating to local events and some of the "wanderings" taken by Bath Road men during the course of their railway careers.

I wonder how many passengers travelling to and from the capital city in the comfort and safety of the High Speed Trains are aware of an act of bravery that happened on that line just over one hundred years ago. An act of self sacrifice that was to become front page news throughout the country. John Chiddy a native of Hanham was employed as a foreman at a local quarry and on that day in March 1876 he had been working in the siding between tunnels number two and three. The distance between the tunnels being some 400 yards. Walking along the lineside John noticed a large stone which by some means or another had fouled the line. He knew that the "Flying Dutchman", the crack London to Bristol express would come speeding through at any moment.

There was not a minute to spare so without hesitation or thought for himself John made a dash for the stone and with a superhuman effort he managed to wrench it free. Unfortunately the express train came roaring out of the tunnel at fifty miles per hour, hitting John and killing him instantly. Every newspaper in the United Kingdom commented upon his bravery. He had sacrificed his life but had saved so many others, for if the train had hit that boulder at that speed a major catastrophe would have occurred. John Chiddy was forty seven years old, he left a widow and eight children, three of which were under twelve years of age.

An appeal for subscriptions for the widow was started and a mere £3.17s

(£3.85) was collected — a poor price for a man's life. Eventually his heroic deed reached the ears of a M.P., one Lord Elcho. His Lordship placed a notice which was heard in full one August evening in the House of Commons. Part of Lord Elcho's stirring speech contained these words. "Bravery in the field is recognised by the Victoria Cross and bravery at sea by the Albert Medal and if a civilian is called upon to perform an act of bravery it ought to be recognised, and if he risks his life he ought to do so with the conciousness that his family would not be dependant on charity or the workhouse". Humble John could have never dreamt that one day his name would be read out in the halls of the exalted.

Lord Elcho's words did some good and stirred some action in certain quarters. Prominent citizens of Bristol called a meeting to organise a memorial fund. A circular was issued and a sum of £500 was raised. This included a donation from the Baron and Baroness De Langer of Prussia. It was decided to purchase a plot of land at Hanham and to erect a cottage upon it. The completed building would then be presented to John's widow and children. This was done and in 1877 the Chiddy Memorial Cottage was built on a spot from which a clear view could be gained of the place where brave John gave his life that bleak afternoon.

The key of the house was handed over to the widow with due ceremony on January 8th 1878. The Wesleyan and National Schools were closed for the day and close on 300 children gave attendance. A procession was formed and proceeded to the house. A tablet was unveiled by Mr. Whitwell with these words "Many heroes often gain honour at the cannons mouth and get glory by destroying the lives of their fellow men, but God's heroes often gain glory by saving the lives of others, John Chiddy was one of these heroes". The ceremony closed with the band playing "Home Sweet Home".

The tablet bearing the following inscription is on the north wall of the cottage and can still be seen today, it reads "Erected AD 1877 by public subscription for the widow and family of John Chiddy who was killed by an express train whilst removing a large stone from the metals of the Great Western Railway near Conham. March 31st 1876". The cottage has since become part of the aptly named Memorial Road. There are two large stones still situated in the area. The first of these is mounted on brick columns and is situated alongside the 'Up' line close to the mouth of St. Anne's or number two tunnel. The other can be found adjacent to the 'Down' side line. This one used to have a smaller object mounted on its top. Local residents say this is a thunderbolt; which ever one of these is connected with our hero, it was indeed a superhum effort.

Generations of steam locomotives have passed through this spot, many of them being brand new ones on running in duties from Swindon Factory. Over the years the cry of their whistles have become familiar through the tunnels.

Such a sound was to be the last John Chiddy heard on this earth as he struggled to move that obstacle with an express bearing down upon him.

Staying with the local scene I would now like to relate the story of a once familiar figure on the railway scene. This was Miss Emma Saunders whose little chapel was situated in Mead Street. This building was frequently used by Bath Road firemen when attending their improvement classes. These men gave up their spare time to learn the necessary skills for passing out as drivers. In Emma's chapel they brushed up on their rules, they learnt how to read the motion and all about the "ins and outs" of the steam engine. These men were not paid for attending these classes, they went because they were dedicated men.

Miss Emma was a regular visitor to both St. Philips Marsh and Bath Road shed. She could be seen handing out her bible texts to members of staff. The usual cursing often associated with engine sheds was missing when this lady went on her rounds. Railway men of all grades showing great respect towards her for her good work. She had helped many retired men who had lost their wives through death, and through no fault of their own had become down and out. When Miss Emma herself passed away, her kindness was not forgotten. A plaque was unveiled in her memory which reads "Born 1841. Died 1927. Miss Emma Saunders the Railwaymen's Friend. Erected by railway workers and friends in grateful remembrance of her fifty years devoted Christian service".

The plaque which can be seen outside the main entrance at Temple Meads station seems also to be a favourite with nature, for growing above it is a healthy bunch of ferns. The only place on the whole of the station approach where such growth can be found. The little chapel in Mead Street fell out of use in later years, but it survived to the end of the seventies. Although looking somewhat weather beaten, the name over the door still proudly read "Temperance and Railway Hall". When the first part of the Pylle Hill goods depot was demolished in December 1979 Emma's little chapel disappeared with it. Another link with the steam age had been lost forever.

Like the railway, the surrounding district has seen many changes. The steep little streets with their rows of houses have disappeared. These were the homes of the drivers, firemen and guards, many of these dwellings were used as double home lodges, the GWR favouring private houses as opposed to hostels, which were widely used by the other railway companies. One of the local public houses had a wonderful array of steam locomotive photographs adorning its walls. A tobacconist kept a row of chairs outside his shop so that men from St. Philips Marsh could enjoy a smoke and a chat in comfort before going home. Those steep and narrow streets no longer ring to the footsteps of railwaymen coming and going at all times of the day and night. Gone too is the once familiar sight of the callboys riding around the district on their bicycles. The work involved with the steam locomotive was not only a job it was a way of life.

My search for information has taken me into the homes of many railwaymen, some of whom were retired. These men had seen service on the 'Dukes', they had fired the 'Barnums', the 'Bulldogs' and the 'Flowers'. They had witnessed with great joy the coming of the 'Halls', the 'Castles' and the much loved 'Grange' class. As young cleaner lads they had seen the passing of the graceful 3031 'Achilles' class and in later years the demise of the rough riding 4-4-0 'Counties'. They remembered with affection the speedy 'Cities'. One of the class which always arrived at Bristol early with the 'Down' London was the fleet footed *City of Truro*. Many's the night I have spent with these men looking back over their careers. Many of them were in the twilight of their lives, quite content with their gardens or tending to their allotments, but a gleam would appear in their eyes as they recalled tearing through Hullavington at one hundred miles per hour, once again these men would feel the regulator in their hand and the swaying footplate beneath their feet, once again they would hear the roar of the exhaust and the singing of the injector.

Most of my informants had seen service at other sheds and some on other railways, Ron Hacker now a top link diesel driver started his career as a cleaner at Andover Junction, on the old Midland and South Western Junction Railway which was known as the "smack". During the early GWR regime the "Duke" class was prominent here. No 3285 *Katerfelto* being well remembered. Ron saw service at Frome and Swindon before coming to Bristol, where he worked his way through the links at St. Philips Marsh and Bath Road sheds as both fireman and driver. Another engineman with a varied career behind him is retired driver Norman Anderson. During the early days of amalgamation sixteen men were sent from Bath Road to work on the Taff Vale Railway, Norman being one of these. He soon found out that on this newly formed GWR territory that old habits die hard. He was on a 'Down' coal train when his driver told him to pin down the brakes on the wagons, to comply with incline instructions. On the GWR this duty was always carried out by the guard and Norman rightly reminded his mate of this. After a while the now irate guard had come forward and pinned down the brakes. After which he made a point of telling this "visitor" from the GWR that he was now working on the Taff Vale and would abide by *their* rules! His other memories of the Taff was that it had signals everywhere and the amount of coal trains coming down the valleys heading for the docks was colossal. One stretch of the line being known as the Golden Mile. His general impression was that the Taff Vale was a wonderful railway. As a point of interest a few of the other Taff Vale rules included, Rule 12 "Every person to come on duty daily, clean in his person and clothes, shaved and his shoes blacked". Rule 277

"All persons, especially those in uniform to keep their hair cut". Rule 428 "No person can become a station master, unless he is married".

Engineman Anderson also saw service on the Ex Neath and Brecon Railway, which was known locally as the "Nuts and Bolts" railway. Here he was paired with an elderly driver who sported a long white beard. This driver was due for an eyesight test and Norman knew that his mate's eyesight was not exactly A1. On the appointed day a local inspector arrived at the shed to carry out the said test. After a few colour checks he asked the driver to describe what he saw in a certain chosen area. The driver's description was very accurate, he vividly described a large tree and then went on at great lengths as to what a certain young girl standing beneath it was wearing and all this being at a long distance.

The inspector was greatly impressed with all this and pronounced the driver's eyesight to be satisfactory. After he departed the driver let Norman in on his secret. The young girl standing beneath that tree was the driver's grand daughter and she had been standing there all morning. That's why he had chosen that direction! It was a good job that during these early days such men were not sent to the mighty Swindon for an eyesight test. The N & B shed was situated next to a brewery and over the Christmas period most of the staff went next door to pay their respects and get their just rewards. One duty Norman recalled was the moving of a locomotive named *Gallo* from Neath to Danygraig. This engine was so small that every time she required firing on a journey she had to be stopped and the driver had to leave the footplate. The shed at Danygraig started its life with the Rhondda and Swansea Bay Railway, this company rejoicing in the name of the "Run and Shove Behind".

This system of leaving one's home shed to gain seniority saw Bristol men going to Tondu, Duffryn Yard and Landore to name a few, whilst men from Neyland, Carmarthen, Fishguard, Barry and Radyr could be found here in Bristol. One fireman went to Aberbeeg where he recalls that the drivers' daughters married the local firemen. Such was the life in the smaller railway communities. One Bath Road fireman whilst at Cardiff fired a boat train right through to Fishguard. That day is still very clear to him. It was on a 'Saint' class engine. He remembers the driver pointing out places of interest to him and a single line stretch of railway at Manor Owen. No lodge could be found for him at Fishguard so he spent the night in the train. The dining car attendant awakening him with a full cooked breakfast. This gesture of goodwill being organised by the Fishguard shed foreman.

When I was firing in the pilot link I was very grateful to the kindness of the elderly drivers. We were green young cleaners just passed out for firing and starting our footplate careers. These drivers were nearing retirement and had years of experience at their finger tips, yet they put up with our mistakes and nursed us through our baptism with the fireman's shovel. My first mate

Charlie Lewis was kindness itself. Perhaps these men could remember their first firing turns and could see in us a mirror image of their younger days. Other men that I met during my quest for information included Charlie Iles, he finished his career as a driver on the "Bristolian" duty. Charlie was a member of the first cleaning gang that went to the then newly opened St. Philips Marsh shed in 1911. One of the his favourite engines in those days being 'Duke' class *Isle of Tresco*.

Fred May was another character who was well remembered for his tin of snuff which he always carried in the pocket of a rather stiff waistcoat which held more than one pint of Swindon oil in its material. There were others that I never met like Ernie Richardson who called all and sundry "me old sunbird", and Alex Steele, Ted Hibbard and Albert Giles. All once familiar names on the roster sheet. Just a few names from the countless others that should be entered in the halls of fame for services rendered on the steam locomotive. One of the depot's celebrities was Luke Bateman who once stood as M.P. for Bristol East.

The steam era finally came to an end at Bath Road on the 12th September 1960. The run down of the shed had been a gradual one until that last day when existing staff and locomotives were transferred to the nearby St. Philips Marsh shed. It was a sad day when the demolition men moved in and unceremoniously started to tear down the coal stage and remodel the shed to meet with the needs of the growling diesel. One evening shortly after closure I took a stroll down May Walk to pay my last respects.

The workmen had all gone home, the coal stage was a pile of rubble, bricks concrete and ironwork being all that was left of the place where men had sweated and toiled at their labours. This is where they had shovelled, bent their backs and tipped the drams to replenish the tenders and the bunkers beneath them. Never again would we hear the clatter of the tip, for now it was a memory. The shed had been stripped of its roof and its walls were gone, just the bare framework remained standing. A few solitary looking smoke chutes lay on the floor. The two stationary boilers had been ripped out, never again would their long chimneys emit smoke over the local area and its residents.

It was so silent everywhere, there was not a single railway man in sight and the once familiar scene of activity was missing. The yard where 'Halls' and 'Castles' were prepared was as quiet as the grave, the air of excitement, the steam and smoke and the everyday sounds of an engine shed were now a thing of the past.

Standing there that tranquil evening it was not too hard to cast my mind back to happier times. The Sunday evenings with the shed packed solid with engines, 'Stars' and 'Saints' on the coal road, a 55xx being turned on the table or old 2072 shunting the coalfield.

Then as if to remind me that steam was far from dead a 38xx class burst from under the bridge heading for South Wales with a string of empty wagons chattering noisily behind her. I consoled myself with the fact that both St. Philips Marsh and Barrow Road sheds were still with us. Perhaps they would live on as havens of steam. Of course at this time I did not know that within a mere five years steam traction in Bristol would be but a memory.

The sixties period was to see many changes within our railway network. Not only was the steam locomotive to disappear, branch lines, stations and services would also come under the axe. A man named Dr. Beeching would see to that. Some stations would become unmanned halts, one of my old haunts, Bedminster becoming one of these. It was during the winter of 1979 that I went to revisit the station, only to be greeted by a scene full of sadness. The station buildings have long since vanished. Today very few footsteps echo through its once busy subways. Gone are the flowerbeds and the trolleys which once rumbled along the platforms.

The subway walls have become the target of the mindless graffiti artists, their slogans cover everything. Now a mere ten trains call at the station during the week whilst six call on the Sabbath. My mood of remorse was suddenly broken for there on the subway wall my eye caught a reminder of happier times, painted in large black letters with an arrow pointing to the 'Upside' platform was the name "Weymouth".

In a flash my thoughts turned the clock back twenty years to a warm Sunday morning, the laughter of excited children off for a day by the sea filled

Prairie tank 5186 outside Bath Road Locomotive Factory, 12th September 1960, the day the shed closed its doors to steam traction. *(L.C. Jacks)*

the air. Buckets and spades clutched tightly in their hands. Their parents were laden with shopping bags full of sandwiches, lemonade and flasks of tea. This would be consumed on a sunny beach later in the day and would help to quell an appetite brought on by the sea air. Memories came flooding back of a 'Hall' class engine waiting patiently for the travellers to board her train. The steam whisping from her safety valve and drifting over the rows of houses. By the time she had left Temple Meads her train would be packed. The Weymouth excursions were very popular with the travelling public.

I was brought back to reality when a diesel locomotive thundered overhead. I realised how cold it was. The wind whistled down the deserted platforms, blowing leaves and the litter of a modern day world before it. Somewhere in the darkness a board swung and creaked on its hinges. I wondered what Mr. Ball, the former station master would have thought of the desolation, the emptyness. The station he was once so proud of had been lost in the mists of time. I turned for home and only the footsteps I heard were my own as I left that unfriendly scene behind me.

Bath Road shed reopened its doors to diesel traction in June 1962. For the third time in its history another new episode of railway life was born.

The return of steam to Bath Road. No. 7924 Thornycroft Hall, sans nameplates, on display at Bath Road Diesel Depot for the Open Day, 5th June 1965. She had been specially cleaned for the occasion by the staff at Barrow Road shed, demonstrating the spirit of steam was not quite dead. *(D.K. Jones)*